But Deliver Us from Evil

Father Duffy and the Men of Bataan

By

Dan Murr

MURR PUBLISHING

Florida

Murr Publishing

But Deliver Us from Evil,
Father Duffy and the Men of Bataan

All Rights Reserved © 2008 by Dan Murr

Published in 2008 by Murr Publishing
Jacksonville Beach, Florida
www.DanMurr.com

ISBN: 0-9818407-0-1

Printed in the United States of America

Acknowledgements

A special thank you goes to some hacker out there who stole his way into Joyce Faulkner's email address book and started sending out messages. Thank goodness no viruses were attached. But this guy put me on a road that had never been expected, one that led directly to the late Father John Edward Duffy, former pastor of Our Lady of Lourdes Catholic Church in New London, Ohio, and who served as a Chaplain in the U.S. Army during World War II.

Since Joyce sent out apologies for the hacker's emails that eventually faded away, I thought it would be a nice gesture to acknowledge her. That began an amazing series of contacts in which we discovered our paths had come so close to passing but never quite made it. Then she mentioned Billy D. Templeton's book, MANILA BAY SUNSET, his personal experience on the Bataan Death March on the island of Luzon in World War II. Naturally, that brought to mind Father Duffy's ordeal on that same march. He also had been at Clark Field near Manila at the same time as Templeton when the Japanese attacked on 8 December 1941.

That lone contact with Joyce triggered the thought to write about Father Duffy's experiences along that same Highway 7 in Northern Luzon. How that thought started isn't exactly clear, but it doesn't make any difference. It ignited a spark that began the research into Father Duffy's life and in a matter of a few days, Joyce had provided a contact with Father Bob Phillips, who gave me another contact with the Rev. Dr. Richard S. Roper. He had written a book, BROTHERS OF PAUL, a series of stories about chaplains

3

in World War II. In it he devoted a chapter to Father Duffy. Dr. Roper graciously contributed his book plus a little later, a letter that Father Duffy had written to the father of Navy Ensign Jack Gordon, who had died while he worked along side the chaplain in a Japanese POW camp.

My cousin, Bob Farmer who resides in Father Duffy's town of birth, Lafayette, Indiana, also contributed along with the moral support from Lisa Covol, step-granddaughter of Dorothy Vogel Baltes, and my long-time friend Elaine Mellott, both from Norwalk, Ohio.

There also came assistance from Father Bob Thomas, who still resides in Tucson, Arizona and was formerly pastor of St. Paul's church in Norwalk.

Ben Steele, the noted artist and retired professor of art emeritus at East Montana State College at Billings, became even more special. Ben drew pictures while in prison and they constitute one of the most powerful accounts of life as a POW in the Philippine Islands. He also provided his personal experience on the death march, was wounded once when he tried to assist a fellow prisoner. Ben began to develop an extreme hatred for the Japanese during the march and his days as a POW "that lasted way beyond the end of the war," he said. After the war, he attended the Cleveland Art Institute at Cleveland, Ohio and also attended Kent State University. He eventually moved in with Father Duffy at Our Lady of Lourdes Parish at New London, Ohio to assist the noted chaplain and priest in writing a book about his experiences. Father Duffy intended to have Ben illustrate it for him.

The notes taken from the dictation he had given to his niece, Dorothy Vogel, and used in this story were no doubt intended to be used in part of his book, which he never had a chance to write.

Later, after Ben became a professor at the Billings, Montana college, Japanese students became his friends, "And they were able to help me to forgive them so I now have several Japanese friends."

A special thanks goes to my classmate, Vaughn Neel, who originally wrote an article on Father Duffy that was published on the New London, Ohio website. He also furnished additional information

4

from a wealth of files that he accumulated over the years and writes for that website and also for the New London Historical Society that also contributed.

Pete Ueberroth, director of the archives at the Diocese of Toledo, was a tremendous help during my two days there going through Father Duffy's file. He said that the chaplain's file was the biggest of all the priests' files in the archives and that I was the first to have gone through Father Duffy's history in several years.

Three sisters, Janette Filla, Joyce Peters and Ardis Budd, contributed the dramatic story of Father Duffy's death-bed conversion of their father, Pete Clemmons, in 1954.

Information also came from articles in The Chicago Tribune, The Toledo (Ohio) Blade, Fort Wayne News-Sentinel, the Cleveland Plain Dealer and Tippecanoe County Historical Association in Lafayette, IN, and the Wikipedia Free Encyclopedia.

The Louis A. Stokes Veterans Center in Cleveland, Ohio and Military Personnel Records Center in St. Louis, MO also would have contributed, but were unable to because of circumstances beyond their control.

And if anyone has been neglected, please forgive the error for it was not intentional.

A Foreward

From the study hall on the second floor of the old New London High School building back in 1947, you could look out the windows and across the street and see Our Lady of Lourdes Catholic Church. Remodeling had begun and often times Father John E. Duffy would walk around the outside of the old structure to make sure everything was going well and according to plan.

No one talked much about Father Duffy back then and none of the students who belonged to Our Lady of Lourdes Parish said anything, either. Consequently, some of us never knew until later what he had endured as a U.S. Army chaplain in the Philippine Islands where he served during World War II, that he had been captured and was a survivor of the Bataan Death March, that he had been wounded six times, or that he had spent most of the war as a prisoner of the Japanese.

Father Duffy used to spend many Friday nights at the Broome-Wood American Legion Post 292 with other legion members. Once you became aware of his experiences as a chaplain, it was easy to understand his desire to be close to the other former service men who also served during WWII. He was a past commander of that post.

Even though I was a member of the Broome-Wood post, no one ever spoke to me about Father Duffy, maybe because at the time, I was not Catholic. However, the entire village of New London was proud to have him selected as the National Chaplain for the American Legion in 1952.

My father was Chief of Police for the village of New London and knew Father Duffy until he finally had to resign from the parish because of his health issues. Then he moved to Carmel, California and died at Letterman General Hospital at The Presidio in San Francisco on 4 June 1958.

Father Duffy attributed his health problems after the war to the wounds he suffered during the death march and from the wounds he received during the bombings and strafing of the Japanese Hellships.

While doing the research for Father Duffy and the Men of Bataan, a dissertation on the Bataan Death March written by Stanley Lawrence Falk while he was studying for his Masters Degree at Georgetown University in 1952, revealed why Japanese guards were so brutal during the death march.

According to Falk's thesis, the Japanese character at the time of World War II was the result of centuries of violence and treachery, that life on a crowded land was highly competitive and lightly regarded. That did not, however in Falk's view, condone the terrible atrocities that occurred on the death march.

The Japanese soldier's life was by no means an easy one. From the time his military life began, he was subjected to harsh discipline and brutality. He was expected to obey orders swiftly and no questions. Laggards and dissenters were quickly and physically punished.

The first three months of training were the toughest. Recruits who didn't show proper respect, or didn't wash the clothes or clean boots of older or higher ranking soldiers satisfactorily were often beaten into insensibility. Superiors would strike them with an open hand or fist, kick them with nailed boots or beat them mercilessly with rifles, swords or bayonet sheaths. Physical punishment was openly administered to enforce discipline.

To become a prisoner was the ultimate disgrace for the Japanese soldier. To be killed in action or by suicide if found necessary, was preferred to surrender. Thus, that the Luzon Force, composed of American and Filipino soldiers, surrendered most likely increased the severity of their treatment.

Instructions issued to Japanese military men stated that "to be captured not only means disgracing the army, but your parents and family will never be able to hold their heads up again. Always save the last round for yourself."

Suicide in place of surrender was accepted blindly by the soldier. Surrender was such a disgrace that Japanese troops considered it a duty to kill their own wounded rather than to be captured.

Because of the Japanese indoctrination about suicide not surrender, he looked upon an enemy who surrendered with great contempt. Therefore, the brutality he dealt his prisoners didn't seem excessive, so there was little if any compassion for the enemy.

Some American troops, when captured, were offered an opportunity and weapon to commit suicide. When they declined, the Japanese were surprised.

To continue Falk's analysis, Americans and Filipinos that composed the Luzon Force and suffered through the toughest period of fighting on Bataan could never have foreseen the vale of horror they would encounter in captivity.

"The agony they endured, the death they often welcomed was not deviously and maliciously planned. Rather they were the result of four conditions. The first was the incredibly low physical state to which the Bataan defenders had sunk by April 9. The second was the Japanese unpreparedness to receive so many prisoners (70,000) in such condition, their inability to improve this condition and their unwillingness to accept General King's solution of transportation for the POWs. The third was the cruelty and callousness of the individual Japanese soldier whose training, instinct and experience stifled the Western virtues of mercy and understanding. The fourth was the failure of Japanese leadership."

Falk believes that any one of these conditions might have been overcome, but together, they produced the fatal disorganized event that came to be known as the "Death March."

Excessive brutality during the Japanese soldier's training and discipline doesn't excuse his atrocious treatment of prisoners. Such treatment, like physical punishment of fellow troops, is specifically forbidden in Japanese army regulations for the handling of prisoners.

The regulations were presented by the defense in the trial of the U.S. vs. General Homma, the Japanese 14th Army commander that was in charge of the invasion of Luzon.

On Bataan, the disobeying of these regulations was fatal.

The one great desire after completion of the research for this work of nonfiction was to have become more intimate with Father Duffy, to know the man and the priest and his work on much closer terms from my high school days and beyond. There are so many questions that remain unanswered to this day, the answers to which went with him to his grave on that slope inside the National Cemetery at The Presidio in San Francisco.

The Author

Colonel John E. Duffy
Catholic Chaplain, U.S. Army (1932-1946)

(Photo furnished by Diocese of Toledo Archives.)

DUFFY, John Edward

Colonel, U.S. Army – World War II

Date of Birth: 28 June 1899, Lafayette, Indiana

Graduated: Notre Dame, 10 June 1923

Graduated: Mt. St. Mary's of the West Seminary, Cincinnati 1928.

Ordained: 2 June 1928, Diocese of Toledo, Ohio

Date of Death: 4 June 1958, Letterman Hospital, San Francisco, CA

Buried at: Section WS Site 624-E
San Francisco National Cemetery
1 Lincoln Blvd, Presidio of San Francisco
San Francisco, CA 94129

Other POW's pass by after Father Duffy collapses along the highway during the Bataan Death March. A Japanese guard slashes his foot and leaves him for dead.

(Drawing by Sgt. Ben Steele, U.S. Army Air Corps)

Chapter I

A Brutal Beginning

Are they ministers of Christ? (I am talking like an insane person).
I am still more, with far greater labors, far more imprisonments,
far worse beatings, and numerous brushes with death.
~ Paul's 2nd letter to the Corinthians (11, 23)

The squadron commander had already made up his mind. Some Americans were determined not to become prisoners. He and others who had escaped would climb Mount Mariveles up to the Pilar-Bagac road, the main line of resistance against Japanese troops, and join with Filipino guerillas. So the commander began to encounter stragglers that had been separated from their units.

The commander, who had been with the 4th Marine Regiment Air Warning squadron, and six other men grabbed all the cans of salmon and rice they could carry, and in the hot late-afternoon sun of 9 April 1942, began their climb up the mountain.

They all had eluded Japanese troops from around Mariveles the day before the surrender, and now, with the commander in charge, were making their way into the jungle. When they finally stopped, the commander told them, "This is our situation now. We're probably all listed as missing in action, but we can decide for ourselves what we want to do. We can either go back and surrender . . . become prisoners of war, or we can try to get off of Bataan."

They all agreed. Continue to elude the enemy and join the Filipino guerillas rather than surrender.

Their first indication that something had happened that morning of the surrender – bombing and strafing of artillery positions had stopped, and an eerie silence began to settle over Bataan and the town of Mariveles down on the southern tip of the peninsula. It was the morning of 9 April and word quickly spread that Major General Edward King, without orders from his commanding officer, General Jonathan Wainwright, had surrendered some 70,000 Filipino and American troops.

For the first time, they realized that they were alone. No 4th Marine Regiment, no Army, no Navy, only a few rifles and .45 automatics and not much ammunition. Thus, when the small group of men reached the Pilar-Bagac Road, they stopped. Japanese troops were crossing it at steady intervals. Darkness had settled in when the commander began to time the gaps. They waited between the lead enemy group and the following group, and then they'd dash across the road and hide in the tall grass. In the darkness they decided to stop for the night and wait until dawn before moving on.

The commander awoke early, just as shadows of trees began to take shape in the dawn's light. He quietly woke the other men to resume their climb, and just as they started from their hiding place, almost tripped into an area where Japanese troops had bivouacked for the night. They were still asleep. Had the Americans continued on in the darkness the night before, they would have walked straight into the enemy camp.

As they continued their climb up the peninsula and Mount Mariveles, they discovered they were parallel with a long line of prisoners guarded by Japanese troops. They could hear guards yelling and every so often, a gunshot reached their ears. This would become known as the Bataan Death March.

One of the sergeants had not seen his battalion commander since the surrender. It was now the third day and as they continued on, he could see in the distance a soldier tied to a tree. He appeared to be asleep, his head slumped down on his chest. But as they came closer, they could see he had been stripped to the waist; his khaki pants blood-soaked. As they reached the immediate area, it became obvious that the soldier, an officer, was dead, that his body was

16

covered with bayonet wounds. It left no doubt what had happened to the major.

As the small group of men moved on up the mountain, they could see what was happening down on the road to their fellow soldiers – beatings with rifle butts; another soldier fell along the road and was bayoneted; another broke from the line toward water along side the road. He dived head first into the ditch, but before he could drink, a Japanese soldier raced over to him and with one mighty swish of the sword, the G.I.'s head rolled away from his body. It was as if everyone took a deep breath and couldn't let it out, it was such a shock.

The prisoners were already suffering from illness, the tremendous heat, dehydration, lack of food and water, dysentery, and the atrocities by enemy soldiers.

The commander and his small group witnessed more beatings, stealing from prisoners, and some of those who had been killed. The commander recalled seeing two men standing at attention, the hot sun beating down on them and with no water, back at the Mariveles airfield in front of the enemy commander's headquarters. He had seen them standing there in the morning and when he had made his way past the same area again that afternoon, they were still standing there at attention, the sun at its hottest.

A little farther up the road, they saw another group of soldiers. One they recognized as the chaplain from Fort Stotsenburg. He slowly limped along, obviously in pain and not doing well. He finally dropped by the roadside. That brought another Japanese guard to his side. He poked at the chaplain with his bayonet.

"Up . . . up," he ordered and waited to see if the chaplain would obey. He did not. Then the soldier shoved his bayonet into the chaplain's back. There still was no movement, so the guard slashed at his foot to make sure he was dead. He waited a few more moments, and then resumed his duty of guarding the POWs.

Somebody whispered, "Father Duffy."

"Yes . . . yes," another prisoner softly said. "May God rest his soul."

* * *

John Edward Duffy became Father Duffy on 2 June 1928. He had been ordained by the Most Reverend Samuel A. Stritch, who would later become Cardinal Stritch, at St. Francis DeSales Cathedral in Toledo, Ohio.

Father Duffy's parents, James E. Duffy and Sadie J. McDowell, were issued a marriage license on 26 July 1898. On the 27th, they were united in marriage by the Rev. John R. Dinnen in Tippecanoe County, Indiana. Almost to the day, eleven months later, John Edward Duffy was born in Lafayette on 28 June 1899.

Lafayette was a shipping center on the Wabash River in its early days. Across the river is West Lafayette, where later, sprawling Purdue University, which has had a large impact on the economy of both towns, was founded in 1869.

Near the turn of the 19th century, James and Sadie Duffy lived in the town of Lafayette, population slightly over 18,000. Located 74 miles northwest of Indianapolis, the town was named for French General Marquis de Lafayette, who had aided American armies during the Revolutionary War. It became the county seat of Tippecanoe County a year after the town was founded in 1825.

Both of John's parents were Roman Catholic and belonged to St. Mary's Parish in Lafayette in the diocese of Fort Wayne. James became a salesman and Sadie his devoted housewife. Then eleven days after John's birth, on 9 July, he was baptized in St. Mary's Church. He later was confirmed and raised a Roman Catholic.

John attended St. Mary's Parochial School and went on to Notre Dame Preparatory School. From there, he attended Notre Dame and received his Bachelor of Arts degree on 10 June 1923.

After graduation from Notre Dame, he worked a year at Cathedral High School in Indianapolis, Indiana, taught Latin, Science, coached football, basketball and the debating team. He moved to St. Louis University the next year and taught Epistemology, Educational Psychology and Methods of Teaching.

John Duffy felt that his original calling was to join the Holy Cross Fathers at Notre Dame. But on 4 August 1924, he submitted his answers to the Diocese of Toledo as a young man who desired to be accepted as a seminarian. He was in good health, had experienced no illnesses during his youth and there were no hereditary sicknesses

Top: The home where Father Duffy grew up at 1525 Ferry Street, Lafayette, Indiana. (Photo by Robert Farmer, Lafayette, IN)

Bottom: Father Duffy becomes a chaplain and is commissioned a First Lieutenant in 1932.
(Photo courtesy of Diocese of Toledo, Ohio Archives)

from his family. And, "No," he dryly answered, "there never has been any form of insanity in my family."

It might have been a little easier for John to become a seminarian than what the ordinary applicant experienced. He needed his baptismal certificate, a certificate of confirmation, letters of recommendation from his pastor at St. Mary's church in Lafayette and from the rector of the college where he studied. He also needed a list of all the marks he achieved in all branches of study he pursued during his six years of college, and a letter from a reputable physician testifying that he gave John a thorough physical examination and found him to be in good condition. The eighth item was fairly easy. He needed to name his place and length of residence of those places where he had resided for a period of six months or more away from the diocese of his residence or birth after his fourteenth year.

John went on to attend Mt. St. Mary's of the West Seminary at Cincinnati, Ohio. When he reached his theological studies, he began to feel more called to pastoral work than university teaching, so he studied for the Toledo Diocese until his ordination.

Father Duffy embarked on his priestly career at St. Wendelin's in Fostoria, Ohio as a curate – a clergyman in charge of a parish - - and Latin teacher from 1928-29. He transferred to St. Ann's High School at Fremont, Ohio as curate and principal on 8 May 1930; became the curate at St. Charles in Toledo and then curate at St. Ann's, Toledo, in 1931.

While at St. Ann's in Toledo, his life took another turn, perhaps because of a second calling. In 1933, the U.S. Army received applications from volunteers for the chaplaincy, but in the diocese of Toledo, there is no record of why Father Duffy decided to volunteer.

In the "Idea and Entrance" of Phase I on his application, it was stated that his motive to volunteer could have been from a number of reasons: In school during 1914-1918, he was in close contact with Filipinos both at Notre Dame and at Mt. St. Mary Seminary; his contacts with the clergy and chaplains, or it might have been just a natural desire perhaps for adventure.

However, in Father Duffy's first letter from the St. Ann's Rectory on 17 April 1933 to the Honorable Warren Duffey, House of Representatives, Washington, D.C., he wrote, "I have full approval of Bishop (Karl J.) Alter," and added "there are no Catholic Chaplains from Ohio."

From that day in April to 2 November of that year, a series of letters were written about his appointment to the chaplaincy. He had filed an application directly to the Adjutant General in accordance with Army Regulations, and had letters of recommendation from Bishop Alter and two others, plus endorsements from all five Congressmen from the Toledo area.

On 31 August he received a letter from the Adjutant General that he would be accepted for a vacancy in a week or ten days. Father Duffy received word on 19 September from one of the Congressmen that he had gone right to the War Department and received an okay. "I think Father is taken care of alright," he wrote. Then on the 21st, the Adjutant General advised Father Duffy that his candidacy "would be given due consideration."

A month later, on 23 October, Bishop Alter gave Father Duffy permission to take a 10-year leave of absence to become a U.S. Army chaplain, and by 2 November, 1st Lieutenant Duffy had been at Fort Knox, Kentucky about a week. However, he was commissioned a reserve officer rather than his desire to be Regular Army.

(NOTE: If Father Duffy had a special calling in his youth, it was not evident in his files at the Diocese of Toledo, Ohio, the largest file of any of the deceased priests' files in the archives there. No one had gone through his files in many years since he had died in 1958.)

Father Duffy at his quarters.
(Photos courtesy of Diocese of Toledo Archives)

Chapter II
Assignment: The Philippines

After his initial training as a Recruit Chaplain, Father Duffy was transferred to Fort Sam Houston on 8 December 1933 and assigned as assistant division chaplain of the 2nd Division under General Doray. During his duty there, he would meet Fathers Cleary (near San Antonio) and Malmeister (during lent). He spent seven months there, then on 6 May 1934, was assigned to the Philippine Islands and sailed out of San Francisco on the 23rd. Before he headed to San Francisco, he stopped in Toledo to pay his respects to Bishop Alter.

Father Duffy spent three years in the Philippines, first as assistant post chaplain at Fort Stotsenburg, located about 80 kilometers north of Manila near Clark Field, on Luzon. His responsibilities included overseeing the construction of Holy Cross Church at Sapangbato Angeles, Pampanga. He was then appointed its first pastor by the archbishop of Manila, Pedro Santos. He also would have a Filipino assistant.

All of that was completed his first two years at Fort Stotsenburg. Then in August 1937, Father Duffy was transferred back to Fort Devens, Massachusetts. That's where his interest in building new chapels continued despite his heavy workload. In addition to being post chaplain, he assumed the welfare officer's job, became librarian, athletic coach, the Red Cross officer and First Corps Area Chaplain.

When the new chapel was completed in 1939, the Most Reverend John J. O'Hara, D.D. dedicated it, with the Most Reverend Richard Cushing, D.D., the auxiliary of Boston at that time, giving the dedication sermon on 4 February 1940.

Father Duffy had served Fort Devens with distinction, but it came time for him to return to the Philippines. Thus, on 28 April 1940, he sailed again from San Francisco, bound for Fort Stotsenburg. He re-assumed his job as post chaplain and his building projects would continue.

In 1940, the Philippines were the only Catholic nation in the Far East. It had two archdioceses, 10 dioceses and two prefectures (administrators). Of the 10 bishops, seven were native and three foreign. Of the 1,400 priests on the islands, 800 were natives. Eighty-two percent of the 14 million people belonged to the communion of the Faith.

Father Duffy's first project was to build a stone church at Wardville Angeles, Pampanga. That would take from November 1940 until April 1941 and would be dedicated by Archbishop Santos, the archbishop of Manila, on 15 August. It would be named Our Lady of Lourdes, and all military elements there participated in the dedication.

However, it wasn't as easy as it might sound. The church was built in the village of Wardville, a large barrio on the reservation for soldiers and their families. The building, a Spanish mission design of cobblestones, is one hundred feet long and only thirty feet wide. Cobblestones also were used to build three altars and the communion railing. Cement, the roof and windows were purchased, but the labor was donated. The post soldiers donated enough money for the necessary materials.

"I think we got a little of the Catholic spirit that went into the construction of the great churches of the Middle Ages into the building of the Wardville edifice," Father Duffy said in a letter to Bishop Alter.

"The ceiling must yet be completed and the painting will come one of these days. About two thousand pesos have so far gone into the structure," he continued, "but that's nothing compared with what we have. Nothing has gone into the building that we have not paid for beforehand.

"God has been very good to us. Whenever we needed money for something and didn't know whether we could make the next venture or not, something always happened to provide us with the wherewithal.

"Last Sunday I asked for a chalice, a new missal and altar cards, and a ciborium," Father Duffy said. "Mass was scarcely over and I not only had the money for these things, but enough to get two new statues. It's almost unexplainable how good God has been to us and how He has taken care of us."

Although the church hadn't been finished yet, Father Duffy began to use it on a daily basis during the month of May. "I have dedicated it to Our Lady of Lourdes," he said. "It's packed every morning for Mass and at 5:30 each afternoon to pray the rosary, litany and Benediction. We're asking Our Lady to take care of us, and we dedicated these May services to the Holy Father's prayers for a just and lasting peace."

Meanwhile, the strength of Fort Stotsenburg was doubled in February, and Father Duffy asked for and received permission to offer three Masses on Sundays. The extra Mass was a Field Mass at which about 1,600 men attended.

Father Duffy also told of his efforts to attract the greatest number of men to make their Easter confession and Communion during Holy Week.

"Brigadier General Edward J. King Jr., a Protestant, a southerner, and a real gentleman of the old school, gave me his fullest co-operation even to the extent of declaring a free afternoon for confessions," Father Duffy said. About 850 men went to confession. Of those, about 200 were making their first confession.

On Holy Thursday, there were three regiments totaling 3,300 men at Field Mass.

"The general, his staff and many officers were in attendance," Father Duffy said. "The regimental colors and guidons were flying and 850 soldiers received Holy Communion."

Father Duffy said that he's expecting two assistants on the next boat.

He spoke of the interest of Bishop Santos of Naga in establishing parochial schools in his diocese which, Father Duffy said, "is very poor. He's seeking to have sisters from the United States take on the work in some of his schools with a view to establishing a branch of their community in his diocese."

Father Duffy said that Bishop Santos' effort is "an undertaking that's very necessary if the faith of these Catholic people is to be preserved."

The next project was the building of a hospital chapel at Fort Stotsenburg. That was finally completed in June 1941. Then over at Clark Field, construction began for a new post chapel. Only there would be a major disruption. Father Duffy's life and those of American and Filipino forces on Luzon would never be the same again.

Father Duffy (4th from right) at a ceremony at Fort Stotsenburg.

(Photos courtesy of Diocese of Toledo Archives)

(Pearl Harbor Images from Wikimedia Commoms - Public Domain)

Chapter III
Preliminaries to an Invasion

For most of those who were alive at this time in history, December 7th, 1941, will always be a day that lives in infamy. For some, that Sunday will be even more impacted on their minds. They will come to know the enemy better than anyone else. Especially those on Bataan and Corregidor. Father John Edward Duffy will become one of those unfortunate warriors.

When the message arrived that Pearl Harbor had been bombed on 7 December, everyone on Luzon, especially at Fort Stotsenburg and Clark Field, knew that soon, the Japanese would arrive in the Philippine sky.

Early in 1940 a war setting had actually begun to take place at Fort Stotsenburg. *Female dependents of U.S. Navy personnel were ordered back to the United States aboard the transport ship Washington. Then dependents of British military personnel were evacuated in July of that year. In February 1941, orders were issued to make it mandatory for dependents of U.S. Army personnel in the Philippine Islands to be evacuated. To most at Fort Stotsenburg, this was a clear indication that something major was about to happen.

This marks the beginning of Father Duffy's dictation to his niece, Dorothy Vogel, of 66 pages of notes about the preliminary to the Japanese attack on Clark Field and the invasion of the Philippine Islands.

The situation became even more intense when embargoes were placed on shipments of oil, scrap iron and gas in the summer of 1941 and all Japanese credits and money in U.S. possessions were frozen. This action created extremely strained relations between the government of Japan and the United States, Great Britain and Dutch Colonial governments in the Far East.

Representatives of British and Dutch armies and navies came to Manila for conferences and American officers visited fortifications and installations of the British and Dutch.

The Philippine Island Scout Division also was brought up to full strength by the induction of some seven thousand scouts in March 1941 and accompanied by a building and housing program for them.

Six months later, an anti-aircraft battalion of the 200th Coast Artillery arrived from the Philippines, followed by the rest of the outfit in October.

A battalion of tanks of the 192nd Tank Battalion, an Army National Guard unit from Wisconsin, Illinois and Ohio, arrived also in October, and in November the 19th Ordnance Company accompanied that battalion.

Temporary barracks were erected in the vicinity of Clark Field to house these units, and this destroyed the normal type of topography. High-ranking officers believed this construction made the area stand out like a sore thumb.

At the same time, construction also began of several new airstrips, and the regular road to the post was closed in order to build some strips across it. A new road to the post was constructed that followed the railroad tracks along its south side and moved in a westerly direction to the main station. It turned right at that point, cut across to the former road and met at the junction formerly known as Murrayville. At the time Murrayville was occupied by the Air Corps' Non-Commissioned Officers Club.

New barracks also were being constructed between Murrayville and the post hospital to be occupied by tank personnel. Then plans were under way to construct additional quarters at the site of the post golf course. These buildings were expected to house an infantry division that was expected to arrive from the United States in December or January.

"It was my opinion," said Father Duffy "and the opinion of several others that construction of these buildings was a serious mistake. It changed the topography of the ground and made the post stand out. Previously, due to the natural foliage and tropical growth through the years, the old post of Fort Stotsenburg could only be discovered with difficulty from the air.

"In fact," he continued, "the only land mark for locating the fort was the Philippine Islands' training camp."

From May 1941 on, the compliment of officers increased with each incoming transport vessel. Some were necessary to meet the needs of the Philippine Island Scout Division. Others would be used to assist in training various components of the Philippine Islands Army.

Included among these additions were chaplains, two of whom Father Duffy received on 8 May and another on 26 June. Chaplain Frederick Howden Jr. arrived with the 200th Coast Artillery Anti-Aircraft group, and Chaplain Joseph LaFleur arrived with the 19th Bombardment Group in November. Three chaplains were assigned to units – Matthias Zerfas to the 26th Cavalry, John Wilson to the 24th Field Artillery, and John Joseph Curran to the 88th Field Artillery.

Also during 1941, Father Duffy received a promotion to major. At the request of General Jonathan Wainwright, Father Duffy was named Force Chaplain, Northern Luzon Force, by General Douglas MacArthur. He held that assignment only until 9 January 1942 when he became Chaplain, First Philippine Corps. He served in that capacity throughout the Northern Luzon and Bataan campaigns.

Between October and November of 1941, fifty-four B-17s arrived at Clark Field via the Pacific route. The first nine of these flew in about the middle of October. There were rumors of their arrival beforehand, but it was all shrouded with secrecy.

"Captain Ray Herrick, who lived with me and was the Signal Officer, knew all about it, but refused to comment. He wondered how

I had heard about their arrival," Father Duffy said. "I asked Herrick if he didn't want to go down to see them come in. It was a very rainy day, visibility almost zero, but he agreed to come along."

They parked back of the Operations Building and went inside where they met General King and several other officers of the post who had arrived to witness the landing of the Flying Fortresses.

"Everybody felt a little sheepish at meeting the general there because the arrival of the planes was supposed to have been very very secret," Father Duffy said. "As I recall, their arrival filled us with a great deal of pride. It (the B-17) was considered the best battle plane in existence at that time and the longest range bomber."

General King and all the officers watched the B-17s land without mishap, except that one B-17, in taxiing to its parking place, swiped its tail on a truck and knocked the rudder off. The pilots also were under orders not to radio anything home about their trip.

Captain Herrick had considerable difficulty with some of the young aircraft officers. He refused to send some of the messages they wished sent back to the U.S. contrary to an existing order.

"Old Ray, in his inimical manner, reminded them that they weren't here because they had just flown the Pacific . . . that we did that every day now . . . they needn't think they were second Lindberghs," Father Duffy said and broke a little grin.

While their arrival was supposed to have been secret and there was to be no talk, especially with civilians or any other nationals, true to the undisciplined tradition of the Air Corps, this meant nothing.

"Only a night or two later, Ray Herrick and I were enjoying an evening in Manila. After the necessary libations and a filet mignon at the Army and Navy Club, we dropped over to Jai Alai to witness Spaniards batting a ball about with a glove called a Pelican Hand, an elongated wicker type, curved glove that's fastened to the wrist.

"The place was filled by the young members of the 14th Bomb Group, and in their enthusiasm of youth and in the fervor of their imaginations, they revealed to the few feminine Americans who," Father Duffy said "tarried behind, their conquest of the Pacific Ocean in America's greatest air weapon, the Flying Fortress!"

Clark Field 1938
(Public Domain Image)

The airmen were consumed by the pleasing mestizo of Spanish charm -- the light brown with a mixture of Malay and Chinese and the chocolate yellows and who always seem to appeal in a pleasing manner to a color known as Drake,

"We were disgusted!" Father Duffy said. "Not that we would deny them a braggart's recital of his conquest to his lady fair, but primarily because of their utter lack of common sense. Even the most uninitiated neophyte knew the Jai Alai was a rendezvous for every foreign agent in Manila, and if they weren't able to gather our military movements from things that were said there, they were dumber than the Sphinx of Egypt.

"Ray and I were convinced that if anything ever broke here, we would definitely be up against it," Father Duffy said. "That was because of the apparent impossibility of getting any of the new officers to realize the seriousness and precariousness of the position of the handful of Americans that were on hand for even a token resistance against the military might of the Rising Sun."

Two other instances with reference to aircraft at Clark Field and their lack of military discipline might be exemplified that in October a plane flew in from Iba carrying a boy who had been injured. The plane dropped a flare, then landed and transferred his patient to the hospital without even being challenged by a guard. This necessitated General King's insistence upon further instruction to the guards and the threat of military discipline against the commander of the field if such an incident should occur in the future.

On the second occasion, when a plane dropped a flare and landed, although challenged by the guard, the number of flares dropped and the nature of the air warning orders in force at that time were such that Captain Herrick, who was quite aware of the possibility of enemy action in this theatre, sent an (alert) flash to Manila: "Unknown plane overhead, dropping flares in vicinity of Clark Field, direction of coming and going unknown."

Herrick received some unwarranted kidding. and the nickname "Flash," was attached to the captain. Father Duffy said, "What we needed were many more people who had a similar irritation to the signal corp captain who shared quarters with (what some called) the war-mongering padre.

"In late November, Captain Herrick was routed out from my quarters at all times of day and night to decode special messages that were coming from Washington," he said. "I was anxious about the contents of them, but never could find out anything from Captain Herrick. I suspected they were of a serious nature.

"On 26 November, we were put on an alert status," he continued. "I pre-supposed that this was the result of these messages. What instructions the various regimental and unit commanders received, I do not know. However, all leaves were cancelled as well as all passes to the annual Army-Navy 'Hoopla' (football game) in Manila and arrangements were made to get a remote control broadcast of the game to the Fort Stotsenburg Officers Club."

Herrick continued to decode messages that came in between then and 7 December. "He continued to be routed out on several nights to translate these coded messages," Father Duffy said. "I began to pick up rumors from other sources to the effect that we could expect an attack from the Japanese at any time. Where and when was not known, but the instructions were not to fire until you were fired upon, unless an attack was necessary for defense of your own installations."

Father Duffy didn't know how true these rumors were, but to him, they seemed sound, reasonable and logical.

"At dinner, I familiarized Herrick with these rumors and he insisted upon knowing where I got my information. Of course," Father Duffy said, "I kidded him. Told him that the padre's information is privileged and he could not reveal the source. I gathered from his reaction that though he would say nothing, these rumors were well founded and I would have wagered that they were based upon fact.

"From whom they came, I cannot at this time recall, but I do know that the Tank officers, National Guard officers and the Air Corps officers had heard similar rumors," he concluded.

General Edward P. King had been in command of Fort Stotsenburg since November 1940, but was relieved of his duties on about 28 November and also command of Northern Luzon Force. General Wainwright was ordered to Fort Stotsenburg from the Philippine Island Division at Fort McKinley to assume command of the Northern Luzon Force while King was re-assigned to the staff of General MacArthur as chief of Field Artillery.

General Parker took over command of the Southern Luzon Forces, General Luff took command of the Philippine Island Division, and General Moore became chief of the Coastal Artillery and commander of the Subic Bay and Harbor defenses.

"Those of us at Fort Stotsenburg who knew General King and had served with him since his arrival in the islands," Father Duffy said "knew of the thoroughness of his training programs. He had done meticulous work in building up the defense plans for Northern Luzon, we saw the manner in which he had ingratiated himself with the Filipinos, both military and civilian in the area, and of the confidence that the Filipinos had in him. Most of us regretted the decision of the higher headquarters.

"Some at first were of the opinion that it was done to give him a favorable theatre in which to operate even though little had been done for defensive operations in the Southern Luzon theatre," Father Duffy said.

However, Father Duffy observed, it must be stated that the commanding officer of the 31st Infantry and Colonel Bob Lindsay, of the Field Artillery, while not the potential commanders of the Southern Luzon Theatre, "had done considerable work in that area during the year preceding the conflict. This was fortunate in that later, the command of this theatre would revert to Colonel Jones, later Brigadier and Major General, due to the fact that its commander was never found in that area during hostilities."

USAFFE Headquarters had been established in September with the ordering of Major General Douglas MacArthur (retired) to active duty with the rank of Lieutenant General with the supreme command in the Philippine Islands Department. General George Grainerd was still left in command of the P.I. Department, but this was a rather unfortunate setup. It's believed that even General Grainerd was ordered home to assume command in the U.S. during the latter part of 1941, and that order should have been issued at the time the command was given to MacArthur.

These were the old headquarters, the P.I. Department command and the USAFFE. Most of the P.I. Department chiefs were left in what would compare to service commands of the U.S. and, with the exception of Colonel Willaby, who had been G-4, P.I. and became G-2 in USAFFE.

The rest of the staff was new blood. Dick Sullivan was promoted to Brigadier General and chief of staff of USAFFE, and Colonel MacArthur to chief of staff of P.I. Department.

There were those, according to Father Duffy, who wished that Greinerd had remained and who affirmed that they would rather fight under Greinerd. There were others, he said, who thought that MacArthur was the man of destiny and that the necessary harmony between the P.I. Army and American Army would be much better cared for under his leadership.

"Both were exceptionally good men," Father Duffy said. "It's my opinion that those who failed to appreciate MacArthur did so due to their sole lack of knowledge of him. As head of the P.I. Army and a retired officer, there was no reason why anyone should have very close contact with him. As a result, they didn't know him because of the necessary distance between him and themselves. General Greinerd, on the other hand, was a grand old cavalry general who had always been close to his men and to his officers. He was always a grand old daddy to everyone and, of course, it was only natural that they should resent daddy being pushed out on a limb."

**Father Duffy (center) reads during a
funeral at Fort Stotsenburg.**
(Photo courtesy of Diocese of Toledo Archives)

Chapter IV

Father Duffy's Deep Suspicions

Father Duffy was quite aware that His Excellency, Manuel Quezon, president of the Commonwealth of the Pacific Islands, blamed President Roosevelt and the American people for failure to build up an adequate military defense for the commonwealth in a speech delivered at the University of the Philippines on 5 December 1941. Quezon disclaimed any responsibility for the lack of preparation of the Philippine Army.

Of course, in Father Duffy's opinion, it was necessary for Manuel to have some alibi for his failure to use the re-process tax that was returned to the Philippine government by the U.S. to buy the necessary machinery to defend their country. He made no mention of the fact that he had utilized this money to build several beautiful government buildings. It had been utilized to build Quezon Avenue, Quezon Bridge, Quezon City (the land in Quezon had been purchased by Quezon personally for 10 centavos a square foot) but it was sold back to the Philippine government by Quezon for 250 centavos a square foot and then resold for other projects. It's claimed, Father Duffy said, that Quezon netted a small profit of $25 million on this deal.

The money realized therefrom, he said, is supposed to be deposited in a bank in Argentina. "This was just pin money for Manuel," Father Duffy said. "He had $25 million tied up in Spain that Franco refused to allow him to spend outside the Ibernian Peninsula. And 25 million more in a bank in Hong Kong, plus more in the U.S., and it's affirmed that he could write a check for that much in a London banking house.

"He also claimed that Roosevelt had failed to send him tanks, guns, airplanes, munitions, mosquito boats and other machines of war, that they were a helpless nation and would be unable to defend themselves even though they had a will to fight.

"The affect of the speech was like lighting a fire to a stick of dynamite that blew the lid off of hell," Father Duffy continued. "We felt that an attack was imminent, that Quezon, with his Malay instincts, had some inside dope, even that he knew when and where the attack would come. Some even thought that he was in league with the men of Hirohito. He had been a very intimate friend of a Japanese contractor who for a number of years had lived next to St. Mary's and St. John's Episcopal Cathedral.

"He supped with him at least once a week, but the citizen of Japan, who had a very profitable business in Manila, had left for his homeland some months previously," Father Duffy said. "And there were those, too, who suspected that Manuel might have had some arrangements with the Imperial Household."

Admiral Kichisaburo Nomura and Mr. Saboru Kurusu, special Japanese Envoys, were in Washington, D.C. carrying on peace conversations, but they had failed. Quezon, Father Duffy said, had entertained Kurusu when he passed through the Philippines and made a speech late on a Friday evening.

The stock exchange in Manila was only open on Saturday for two hours, from 9-11 a.m. There were those who thought of closing out their stocks, but did not. They believed that the pulse and vibrations could better be evaluated over a weekend of ruminations. But the stock exchange was never to open again.

During the summer of 1941, Father Duffy learned through the Maryknoll Padres in Manila that the Japanese government had insisted that bishops who were Japanese citizens rule all the dioceses of the Catholic Church in Japan. They had demanded the removal of all foreign-born bishops in the various sections of Japan and had insisted that all church property must be held in the name of Japanese Catholics.

40

This necessitated the removal of several American bishops. Thus the missionaries there encountered considerable difficulty and embarrassment when the Apostolic Delegate Manila yielded to all the Japanese demands.

Father Duffy passed this information on to General King for whatever military value it might have because to him, it was the indication of an organized plan and definite move on the part of the Japanese government toward some large-scale anti-American movement.

In November 1941, Major David Lann came to Fort Stotsenburg on his way back to Washington after a six-month detail as an observer with Britain on the Libyan front. Dave was authorized to visit the Manila area and gave the officers of the post a lecture on his experience at that front. His presence was of particular interest to Father Duffy because the two had served at this post together some six or seven years before and had many interesting friendships while he was there. They had become close friends.

"Dave was suddenly ordered back to the states to accompany Kurusu and an unknown American on the China Clipper (passenger seaplane)," Father Duffy said. "After his departure, I learned that the unknown American was Bishop James Walsh of Maryknoll, who had spent some months in Japan.

"It seems," he said "that the Mitsuis and Mitsubishis had been in close contact with the bishop in an attempt to induce him to use his influence to prevent a war with the U.S. that the Japanese Army was intent upon bringing about.

"It also appears that the Mitsuis and the Mitsubishis realized that such a conflict would not only mean the destruction of their own vast fortunes since they controlled most of the wealth in the Japanese Island empire, but the ultimate annihilation of Japan as a world power. They met with the bishop frequently, had secret rendezvous in Tokyo because they feared the Japanese Gestapo and thought police were under the direct domination of the army.

"They induced the bishop to send many cables to the U.S. State Department," Father Duffy said. "They finally induced him to act as their personal ambassador and wished to get him to the U.S. ahead of Kurusu when they learned that the Japanese government had intended to send him on his mission to meet Roosevelt. They chartered a plane and flew him to Hong Kong and financed his trip to the states. He took the Clipper to Manila and they tried to get him out on the Clipper ahead of Kurusu, but he couldn't get aboard without a clearance from the High Command Sayre office.

"The High Command communicated with the State Department and a delay followed, which necessitated Bishop Walsh missing the Clipper he wished to go out on. The bishop and Kurusu found themselves on the same Clipper, which was somewhat embarrassing to both since each knew the other's mission. What happened after they arrived in the states I know only through newspaper accounts."

Around the middle of November rumors began to circulate in the town of Angeles and adjoining civilian communities of alleged abuses of Filipino schoolteachers at the Wardville School and also at the other post school by American soldiers at Stotsenburg.

"Investigators," Father Duffy said, "proved that they were without foundation. General King asked me to investigate the origin of these rumors. Inquiry among the respected citizenery of Angeles pointed that these rumors came from the market place and the Luzon Bazaar.

"It was my conviction," he said "that they were started by Japanese businessmen in the municipality. I'm convinced that this opinion was correct insomuch as over a year later, when I was recaptured as a guerilla and confined in the Jap provost marshal guardhouse at San Fernando, Pampanga, one of the interpreters was the manager of the Luzon Bazaar."

On 3 December 1941, a member of the General Staff of the Philippine Island Army with whom he enjoyed libations in the city of Manila, told him of a conversation that he had the previous Sunday with his friend, Manuel Quezon.

Quezon affirmed that he would be able to do anything that the officers wanted because he had complete control over the USAFFE command and General MacArthur would do anything that he (Quezon) desired.

"My recommendations upon driving back to the post," Father Duffy said "were not too complimentary to the president of the Commonwealth and I felt that Manuel was convinced that he could sell out Douglas with the greatest of ease."

The remarks Father Duffy made about the esteemed president to Captain Herrick at the dinner table that evening were not too complimentary, either.

"Herrick's fears that I might have something convinced me that I was not too far from the truth," Father Duffy said, "because Herrick was in possession of information that he could not disclose to me."

On Saturday and Sunday Herrick and Father Duffy commented to each other about the complete inadequacy of the defenses and the inability of most people to realize the impending danger of attack. They also spoke of the woeful plight of the Philippine Island Army that was being organized; the self-propelled mounts that had been brought to the post on Friday night with cadres just assigned to them, and no one had any knowledge of where the troops could come from to man them.

Father Duffy also commented upon the ease with which they could be wiped out from the air, and the unknown airships that the air corps reported were slipping into their training formations. He mentioned the shift of commanders, reorganization of the various commands, the transfer of Maitland from Clark Field to Manila, the only air corps officer conscious of dangers of attack, and his replacement by Lt. Col. Eubanks, who had arrived with the Flying Fortresses (B-17s) as the Tactical Commander. He also mentioned Major Daley as ground commanding officer; the appointment of Colonel O'Connor as post commander and a new green post staff, plus the organization of the Northern Luzon Force command under General Wainwright. Many of his new staff had not yet reported.

"We expressed regret that General King, who knew the Northern Luzon setup, had been relieved at such a time as well as his staff which had spent time in studying the situation," Father Duffy said. "We thought that it certainly was an opportune time for devastating action. We had practically no American troops in the islands. Elements of the 31st Infantry and the 200th Coast Artillery (anti-aircraft) had just arrived and had been sent illegally to the island. They were basically a National Guard outfit augmented with trainees, two battalions of tanks -- the 192nd and 194th, also basically National Guard augmented with trainers, and the 19th Ordnance Company.

These were the only American combat troops on the island of Luzon with the exception of the P.I. Scout Division, which was composed of Filipino regulars.

Of course, there were 3,000-4,000 air corps ground troops and almost 1,000 pilots for less than 200 planes that were scattered in various points throughout the island. Corregidor had two American Coast Artillery Regiments, a company of Marines at Olangapo, another company at Cavite, and the 4th Marines were en route from Shanghai to Manila. They reported from the Yangtze River Patrol that the Japanese had been loading troops along the Yangtze early in November, and that they had passed Jap troop ships and battle wagons en route.

At the Fort Stotsenburg post mass on Sunday, 7 December 1941, Father Duffy said he had no intentions of making any reference to the situation. But unwittingly, "In my sermon reminded the listeners of the necessity of always being ready to meet their God, of being free from sin, for we know not when God would call us, and if we were in the passions of supernatural life, that we need have no fear. I insisted that some of us might not be here tomorrow for we know not the day or the hour when we would be called to give an account of our stewardship. I urged any that desired to come to confession afterward.

"After the usual Sunday baptism, I returned to my quarters and had breakfast. Herrick was waiting for me and we dismissed the comments that had been made in the Manila Sunday Tribune on Quezon's Friday speech when Major Miller and Major K. came in and asked me if I was prophesying some more sudden deaths upon the post," Father Duffy said. "I had made a similar comment on those previous occasions during little more than a year, and I was reminded that during another 24 hours there had been a sudden death

44

Father Duffy holding mass at Fort Stotsenburg post chapel, 1941. (Photo courtesy of Diocese of Toledo Archives)

upon the post. The first had been Sgt. Henme, a very fine Catholic boy who had been to the sacrament that Sunday and fell through the bombay of a B-10 the next Monday.

"The second had been after Easter and at that time, on the next day, one of our boys who had made his Easter duty for the first time in three years was forced to bail out of a plane. The parachute caught on the tail and he had been killed.

"The third," Father Duffy counted "had only been four weeks previous when a B-10, engaged in a night flying exercise, dove into the ground and killed four. The comment was that something was going to happen because of the padre's remarks.

"The tank commander," he continued "expressed their regrets at not being able to get ammunition for target practice. They were allergic to our imminent attack. Major Tharp then joined us followed by Colonel Clint Turner and we all agreed that it looked like something was going to break soon. We commented on the lack of discipline in the air corps and the ease with which the whole place could be wiped out and how a paratroop landing of a surprise nature could be made in the vicinity of Stotsenburg."

They figured McKinley, Cavite and Olongapo could take over the whole island in a few hours.

Colonel Malone dropped in about that time from Tarlac where the 31st Field Artillery was being trained. They had been in training a couple of weeks. Their barracks were scattered all along Highway 13 and water had to be hauled at least 20 kilometers. There were no guns with which to train them and they were trying to teach them how to fire 75 mm. guns from diagrams and the blackboard.

The regiments whose nomenclature ended with 2 were just being organized and those that ended with 3 were not to be organized until 6 January. Father Duffy felt it was a sad and pathetic picture. The typhoon season was almost over and six months of dry weather were ahead. In fact, it was the ideal time, the only time for a lightning attack like that, which had been made in Austria, Czechoslovakia and Norway.

"We knew," Father Duffy said "that the conversations had broken down, that Hirohito's formal reply was to be given to Roosevelt by Kurusu on December 7. We listened to the radio all day, trying to find out their reply. We forgot we were twelve hours ahead of Washington and eighteen hours ahead of Honolulu. We retired that night after the last broadcast a little uneasy."

About 4:30 in the morning, Father Duffy was awakened by the telephone ringing in the quarters next to his. Colonel Mohr, General Wainwright's chief of staff, occupied it.

"I listened to the conversation and knew that Honolulu had been attacked," Father Duffy said. "I heard the various commanders being alerted and waited for the general alert gun to sound, but it never sounded."

He thought it might have been wise not to sound it since it didn't warn the neighborhood and the troops were individually alerted.

Top: The Bataan Penninsula, Philippines.

Bottom: The aftermath of the Japanese attack on Clark Field.
(Public Domain Image)

Chapter V

The Clark Field Attack

It was on 8 December 1941; Father Duffy was scheduled to celebrate the 6 a.m. mass at the hospital and the 7:30 mass at Wardville. The hospital mass started promptly at 6 and he was able to finish and reach his car by 6:30 when the first news broadcast came on. The Philippine Islands are located across the International Date Line, so while the attack on Pearl Harbor came on 7 December, it actually was 8 December in the Philippines and on the way to his quarters, he learned of the devastating damage affected by the Japanese at Pearl Harbor. Upon his arrival, he found Colonel Stanwell, who was to live with Father Duffy and Captain Herrick, had arrived.

"We commented on the damage at Pearl Harbor," Father Duffy said "and estimated that every battleship had been sunk and that most of the Pacific Fleet was wiped out. We decided that the situation was worse than had been depicted over the radio, and wondered when the Nips would strike at the Philippines. We estimated that it would come very soon."

They had noted that the 26th Cavalry was moving and that the field artillery units were lined up to move out in some battle positions. They didn't know their orders and decided they should draw gas masks at once.

Father Duffy and his roommates had their steel helmets and instructed the houseboys to prepare their field equipment so they could move out to the field in a moment's notice.

"Then I proceeded to Wardville and said mass," Father Duffy said. "I announced to the crowded church of Filipino women that we would offer the mass to Our Blessed Mother to help us in the war and to come forth victorious in the conflict in which we were engaged. It was the last time I was to say mass in that chapel until I was a guerilla, when one day almost a year later, with imprudent audacity, I celebrated mass here when the Japs were complete masters of the island and entrenched in command of Stotsenburg.

"But," he said "due to the mercy of God and the vigilance of the Filipinos, we were able to affect this without being detected by the enemy.

"Upon my way home from breakfast, a gas mask was drawn. When I arrived, Mesario (the house boy) informed me the post commander had been trying to locate me for over an hour, so I called headquarters at once and was told to report as soon as breakfast was completed."

When Father Duffy reported, he was informed about the danger of the imminence of attack, the necessity of instructing other chaplains on the post to be prepared for such an encounter.

Upon this occasion, as school officer, Father Duffy requested authority to close the schools and send the children home so they wouldn't be confronted with that responsibility in the event that bombs should drop on the post school building.

Colonel O'Connor, who was new on the post, immediately canceled the request and authorized the closing of the schools. Before Father Duffy could proceed to carry out this directive, an enemy force had attacked Camp John Hay at Baguio. It was estimated that there would be an attack at Clark Field about 9:30.

Father Duffy immediately proceeded to the schools and ordered the children home, then returned to Post Headquarters. He learned that the big bombers had been loaded with fuel and bombs and had been ordered by General Weiss to take off and bomb Jap installations at Taiwan, that the air commander had refused to comply with these orders, had referred them to Headquarters of the Air Corp in Manila, which ordered them to install the bombs and stay on the ground. A total of 27 B-17s had taken off for Del Monte Field at Mindanao on a routine trip.

About 10:15, a report came through that an attack had been made 15 minutes before on warehouses along the railroad at Tarlac.

"I then took Chaplain Brown with me. We went down to the 200th and the 19th Bomb Group to instruct chaplains Howden and LaFleur on the seriousness of the situation, and to tell them to be prepared for action that was liable to come at any time," Father Duffy said.

"We noted a large group of fighter planes on the main runway at Clark Field. But there were no planes in the air over Clark, so we went to the Operations Office and inquired what the orders were. They said they had none.

"We asked why three squadrons of fighter planes were on the runway, a perfect target for anyone who wanted to attack. We were told that they had just come in to be re-gassed and serviced and the trucks were working on them," Father Duffy said.

The pilots were all over at the Bachelor Officers Quarters eating lunch. Father Duffy asked why there were no planes over the field scouting or trying to protect the field. They were met with the answer that they didn't know.

That was about 11:30 a.m. One of the squadrons took off 10 minutes before the attack, but the rest were destined to be caught flat-footed on the ground.

Father Duffy and his roommates proceeded back to the main post and after they checked for any new instructions from post headquarters, returned to their quarters.

Father Duffy was expecting guests for lunch at his quarters, Colonel S.L. James and Mrs. Nesker, who was visiting the islands. Colonel James intended to meet Mrs. Nesker at Fort Stotsenburg and take her to Manila. Due to the developments of the last four hours, Father Duffy didn't know whether to expect them or not.

Mesario, Father Duffy's houseboy, greeted him when he arrived. "Mrs. Nesker has arrived, but we're still waiting for Colonel James."

"I don't think Colonel James will be here," Father Duffy told Mesario. "He's undoubtedly extremely busy in the Manila headquarters."

A few minutes later Mrs. Nesker emerged from the redecoration room and she and Father Duffy introduced themselves.

"What would you like to drink?" Father Duffy asked, and then suggested a Rye Coke.

"That would be just fine," she said.

Father Duffy had learned from the wife of a president of a radio station that Mrs. Nesker was a newcomer to the island, had secured passage over the objections of the State Department and had been enjoying her stay in the islands. She was returning to Manila after a holiday in Baguio, called the gateway to Northern Luzon and the Summer Capital of the Philippines. The city, located in Benguet Province, is 161 miles north of Manila in the hills of the Cordillera Mountains.

Mrs. Nesker had left Baguio prior to the 8:30 attack on Pearl and knew nothing about that, but she had passed through Tarlac after the 10 o'clock raid there, knew of the bombing and had seen the results of the damage to the warehouses there.

She and Father Duffy talked of the happenings in Hawaii and the islands and he said to her, "Something will probably happen here very soon. At least we're expecting the enemy to launch an attack."

They turned on the radio for the 12:30 broadcast, heard a summary repetition of the Pearl Harbor disaster, and were told that Camp John Hay, located at Baguio, and Tarlac along with Clark Field were rumored to have been under attack.

At this interval, which was exactly at 12:37 p.m. by Father Duffy's wristwatch, explosions began to reach their ears from the direction of Clark Field. The attack was actually in progress; sirens screamed across the base, and the alert gun boomed in the distance, sounding the call to arms.

Father Duffy thought, "And here's the Padre, in one helluva fix -- the enemy blasting hell out of the place and a woman on his hands." Then he suddenly realized he must report for action at once although he hated to abandon a woman in distress.

"Mesario," he called, and the houseboy was right there. "I want you to watch after Mrs. Nesker. I think the best place for her is out in the yard, laying flat upon the ground. And you and the other house boys stand by and do the same thing."

"Yes, sir," Mesario said.

The boys stayed with Mrs. Nesker during the entire attack.

Father Duffy, meanwhile, stopped for his steel helmet and gas mask then proceeded to report at headquarters. By this time all the major explosions were over. Two squadrons of heavy bombers had passed over the post at an altitude of about 20,000 feet. They flew from the direction of Pinatubo, a volcano, and traveled toward Mt. Arayat, a solitary volcano to the west in the Zambales Mountains.

The first squadron of twelve twin-engine bombers dropped their payloads on aircraft and buildings just as the air raid siren began to wail. While the 11th Air Fleet's planned attack had been delayed by heavy fog, it had actually caught two squadrons of B-17s on the ground, loading bombs and refueling for an attack that General MacArthur had ordered on Formosa. The 20th Pursuit Squadron had re-fueled and was waiting to take off just as the first bombers appeared over Clark Field. All but one B-17 was lined up on the field.

The second flight of Japanese bombers immediately followed the first flight and remained over the field for about fifteen minutes. With American fighter planes on the ground, enemy bombers were able to carry out their mission without any resistance.

Japanese pilots had achieved total surprise, just as the others had done at Pearl Harbor.

By the time Father Duffy arrived at post headquarters, about thirty-four Jap Zeros, which were believed to be carrier based, roared in on a low-level strafing attack on the B-17s and fully fueled P-40 fighter planes. Only three of them from the 20th Pursuit Squadron managed to take off. Five others were bomb victims as they taxied to the take-off area and five others were caught in the strafing attack. The three that did get off the ground shot down three or four enemy planes, but Japanese Zeros were able to carry on their attack for about an hour.

The enemy Air Fleet's attack on Clark Field was more successful than they had expected. The first flight of bombers had targeted hangars, barracks and warehouses and left them burning. Some of the grounded planes were damaged in the bomb runs, but the majority of casualties were inflicted by the low-level Zero attack. There were fifty-five killed and more than a hundred wounded.

When Father Duffy arrived at post headquarters, Jap fighter planes were roaring in at a low altitude, strafing post targets and in particular the signal corps center. They flew in formation and at distinct intervals in the time that it took a group of them to circle their special areas.

Father Duffy proceeded to Clark Field, which had become the center of activity, and disembarked from his car in the vicinity of the 803rd Engineer Barracks. He left the car under a tree and after he escaped a shower of bullets, ran to the trenches in front of the small air corps officers' quarters.

Tanks parked in the rear were firing their 47 mm. guns at the invaders while the 200th Antiaircraft's 75s and 47s were barking away. A bomb ripped through the center of the 28th Bomb Squadron's barracks; another exploded in the vicinity of the dispensary; one went through the corner of Bachelor Officers Quarters; still another hit the rear of the commanding officer's quarters at Clark. Bombs smashed through all the hangars down the line, and craters were torn in the runways. Fighter planes, caught on the ground, lay in ruins and still burning.

Wounded and dead were strewn all about with Jap Zeros still working over all the American aircraft that couldn't get off the ground or anything that moved. Several bombs also destroyed the temporary barracks of the 200th Coast Artillery.

Chaplain Brown was seen loading wounded into his personal car and driving them to the hospital. In the interim, between the time strafers passed over and their return, Chaplain LaFleur found a spot where he could hear confessions and give the last sacraments. Father Duffy gave absolution and extreme unction to five or six men, and then decided the best place for him would be at the hospital. He could anoint the wounded there as they were delivered, and then serve the greatest number of those able to walk on their own and those also working.

After he reached the hospital, he gave conditional extreme unction at the receiving office to each solder as he was taken out of an ambulance.

"I knew it would be effective for the members of my faith and that it would do the others no harm," he said. "There wasn't sufficient time for inquiry about religions tenets of the wounded. By the time all the injured had been brought to the hospital, the essential religious needs had been met."

As the last of the wounded was transported into the hospital, Chaplains Kern, Zerfas and Wilson reported from their outfits, which had taken the field and were located in the vicinity of the post.

Father Duffy instructed them to visit the wards and designated which one each should cover, then proceeded to the morgue where the dead were being brought and gave general absolution and anointed those whom he recognized as Catholics. He then contacted Colonel Durst and discovered that there were four coffins available and requested grave digging details for cemetery No. 1.

Chaplains Howden and Brown were contacted and they proceeded to conduct an Episcopal, Protestant and Catholic service for the deceased.

The dead numbered ninety-nine – five officers, forty-four enlisted men and fifty civilians, houseboys and launders. About five hundred had been wounded.

"It was the bloodiest and goriest mess I had ever seen up to that time," Father Duffy said.

The decision was made that officers be buried in caskets and enlisted men and civilians in blankets. Officers were buried that evening.

Identifying the enlisted men was a major problem. "In fact," Father Duffy said, "even after having the first sergeants check the dead we had to bury most of them as unidentified Americans."

Major Thorp supplied the detail that dug the graves, and the civilians were buried the next day in cemetery No. 2.

It was well after 5 p.m. when everything was completed. Father Duffy returned to his quarters where Mesario and the little houseboy had faithfully remained. "Most of the servants had taken off after the attack and with the exception of General Wainwright, Colonel Pierce and myself, had no servants," Father Duffy said.

Mesario told Father Duffy that General Wainwright had asked Mrs. Nesker to his quarters and that his aide had called a few minutes before and desired him to call the General's quarters immediately upon his arrival home.

At that time, Colonel Stansell and Captain Herrick arrived at their quarters and along with Father Duffy, all immediately ordered a double scotch apiece. Then they began to discuss the events of the last few hours.

Colonel Stansell and Captain Herrick told how they were on their way to lunch and as they passed headquarters their attention was attracted to two formations of beautiful new planes flying in perfect formation at an altitude of about 20,000 feet. They said they wondered if they were some new type of naval planes that they had not seen before. They continued to watch them as they proceeded in the direction of Clark Field. Then they suddenly realized they were enemy aircraft when bombs started exploding all around Clark. Jap planes had passed over the field once but didn't return. Their bombs had been accurate and wiped out most of the pursuit planes and badly damaged thirteen B-17s by strafing. But there still were fourteen in serviceable condition besides the twenty-seven parked out of sight over at Del Monte.

As their discussion continued and centered on how badly they had been hit, the phone rang. The clerk on the other end of the line called Father Duffy to come to General Wainwright's quarters right away.

It was already dusk and blackout regulations were in effect as Father Duffy entered the general's dining room where black curtains protected the good light that glowed.

"Mrs. Nesker is staying here for the night," the general told Father Duffy. "I'll see that she gets to Manila in the morning."

Colonel Mohr, Colonel Nelson, and Captain Pugh also were there with the general, Father Duffy and Mrs. Nesker. They discussed events of the proceeding hours and attempted to estimate what the future situation might be.

General Wainwright was especially disturbed over the destruction to the Air Force at Clark Field. He also was upset by the fact that Colonel Eubanks had said that he wouldn't take orders from him, a major general. Wainwright had ordered him to fuel up the bombers and take off to attack the enemy and to keep planes in the air to protect and defend the field.

"We commented upon the destruction at Pearl Harbor," Father Duffy said "and the possibilities of relief and help from the mainland. We estimated that the minimum time for help to arrive was from one month to six weeks, and that due to the probable destruction at Pearl Harbor, elimination of the Navy and cutting of our lines of communication, that it was almost impossible to expect assistance.

"We also believed," he continued "that subsequent aerial attacks along with the landing of paratroops in strategic areas would render us helpless within a few days. We also surmised that one must wait and see just how the enemy attack would develop.

"It's my opinion," Father Duffy told the others "that there will be no help, that we're a suicide outfit, and that we'll have to hold the Japs off as long as breath is in us. We should expect no help since there isn't even sufficient equipment for normal training purposes in the States. The homeland must be secured first until the machinery of America's vast industrial system is converted to carry out the war effort and to mobilize the nation for the encounter."

Father Duffy offered a prediction that the war would last at least three years if not five, "and that a few of us will survive, but only after enduring torture as a prisoner of war."

The military plan for defense of Luzon leaned heavily on maintaining control of the City of Manila and entry into Manila Bay. The Bay entry was guarded by the fortress of Corregidor and the fortified islands to the east of Corregidor. The West flank was secured by occupation of the Bataan Peninsula, which lay between Manila Bay and Subic Bay. The plan called for a retreat from the main part of Luzon into the Bataan Peninsula and thus hold the integrity of the Bay and the city. Since control of the peninsula was paramount to success, and entry into the peninsula was limited to water entry across Manila Bay and road access via the land connection to the peninsula, stockpiling of food, medical supplies, ordnance and quartermaster supplies in appropriate bunkers should have been routine during peacetime. This, however, was not the case.

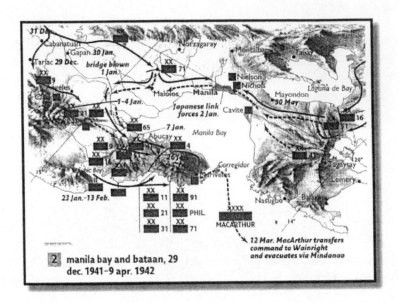

From the start of the Philippines campaign, Japanese forces enjoyed advantages bestowed by possession of the initiative and superior geographical position.

Chapter VI

A Day of Disorganization

Father Duffy, Captain Herrick and Colonel Stansell returned to their quarters and had dinner under blackout conditions. Afterwards, Herrick and Stansell went to headquarters and Father Duffy to the hospital.

As he walked by Colonel Pierce's quarters, he saw that a bus filled with nurses, doctors and corpsmen had parked. They were looking for the hospital, so he pointed out the station to them.

Father Duffy could see that the nurses and doctors seemed pretty well worn, and after a brief discussion, learned that they had been working incessantly. The operating room was in full swing and patients were lined up to await their turn of entry. Both doctors and nurses were to work there all that night and most of the next day in an attempt to save the lives of those injured in the cowardly attack by the Japanese.

After visiting all the wards, Father Duffy proceeded on foot to post headquarters to inquire for further instructions. Since there were none, he returned to his quarters and retired.

At 1:30 in the morning, the telephone rang. Father Duffy was told that enemy bombers were sighted over Northern Luzon headed in their direction and to report to headquarters at once.

"About 2:20, we heard large explosions in the distance," he said. "We estimated that they were bombing either McKinley or Nichols Field."

Subsequent reports proved it to be Nichols. Then at dawn, they could see a large cloud of smoke rising from Clark Field. They later learned that it was one of the pilots in a P-40 taking off on a dawn patrol. He had hit a shell hole and nosed over. He was burned beyond recognition and had to be buried as an unidentified officer since operations could not identify the pilot taking off in that plane.

"The next day, things were much disorganized around Clark Field. Nobody seemed to know if they were coming or going," Father Duffy said. "Some of the troops had gone into bivouacs on the other side of Margot and others were up around the first craters in the Pinatubo area."

The shock of the attack had apparently paralyzed them and no effort had been made to locate the five Jap fighters that had allegedly been shot down. However, a couple B-17s had been sent out on missions to the north and some pursuit planes had been given similar missions.

The place in general was suffering from the previous day's attack. Word came in that Iba, another outlying air field, had been hit and destroyed, that the Japs had followed the pilots in when they returned to be re-fueled and wiped most of them out. Most of the town of Iba was destroyed and also the field. There were very few survivors.

"About 12:30 on the 9th, Cavite was hit and hit hard," Father Duffy said. "I do not recall the number of dead and injured, but it was at least as bad a mess as Clark Field. On the 10th, the Japs got the PBYs just as they landed after an extensive flight. Then between noon and about 12:30, they again worked over Cavite, Nichols and McKinley, attacking in an arch during their operations and doing considerable damage. They met little or no opposition since most of our meager air force had been thoroughly destroyed during the first attack."

On the 9th, the 200th Coast Artillery (anti-aircraft) had been split in two and the 515 men formed and immediately moved to Manila to afford some anti-aircraft protection to that city. On the 10th, with the approval of Colonel O'Connor, Father Duffy set up the Red Cross representative in Wardville and located another branch in the church at Sapang Bato under Father Dayrit to distribute food to the needy soldiers' families.

Mr. Graybill, the Red Cross representative, took charge of these operations and functioned from a house in Wardville.

On the afternoon of the 10th, Father Duffy was sent out by Colonel O'Connor to various towns in the neighborhood to seek the cooperation of Filipino leaders, to calm the people and to locate the Jap planes that had been allegedly shot down.

He located three of the five planes, but the pilots had already been buried. The fuselage and frame of the planes were of metal, but the wings were fabric.

"I cut the numbers off the planes, took some machine guns off them, got insignias and clothing the pilots had worn, which definitely indicated they were Navy based planes, and piled the load into the car," Father Duffy said. "On the way back, I learned there was another plane shot down in the vicinity of Magalong. Upon locating it, I discovered the plane was a B-17 that had evidently been shot down or blown up in the air. Its parts were scattered over about ten acres.

"I learned later that this was the plane that Colin Kelly piloted, that was shot down as he made his approach to land at Clark," he said. "It seems that Kelly had ordered the crew to bail out first and when they cleared (the aircraft), one of the oxygen tanks must have exploded before Kelly got out of the hatch. It probably knocked his head against the hatch and threw him from the plane unconscious. When they found his body, the ripcord of his parachute had not been pulled.

Captain Kelly, from Madison County, Florida, became one of America's first WWII heroes. In a hurry to publicize a rare victory, many Americans believed Kelly and his crew spotted the Japanese battleship Haruna and dropped three 600-pound bombs. They thought one had hit the ship. Actually, the Haruna was not in the vicinity and indications were that the ship was the light cruiser Ashigara, accompanied by a large transport. Some also believed Kelly won the Medal of Honor by diving the B-17 into the smokestack of the Haruna, which turned out to be not true. Thus, the discovery by Father Duffy.

"There were secret papers and maps spread all over the field," Father Duffy said "and a brief case that belonged to Lieutenant Church. I destroyed most of the maps in a fire that I made in the field. The log book, brief case and folded maps were placed in the car. On the way back, I stopped at Linas for refreshments and ran into General Wainwright and his aide who had the same idea.

"They inquired what I had been doing. After I told them, the aide took the keys to the car to inspect the load. He came back quite enthusiastic and after our discussions, General Wainwright inspected the trophies from the fallen plane and ordered me to take them to his headquarters and to tell Colonel O'Connor that he had taken these articles from the fallen enemy planes."

On the 9th, the 23rd Field Artillery had taken up a position on the west end of the parade ground directly in front of post headquarters. Under the command of Captain Fitch, they dug in and prepared to fire muzzle-bursting shrapnel in the event the enemy tried to land paratroops on the parade ground.

On the same day, all the old retired sergeants who lived in the vicinity of Fort Stotsenburg came in to report for duty. About the only troops Colonel O'Connor had was this group of sergeants.

Trenches were dug in the vicinity of Battery A and B barracks and the Signal Corps put in an alternate switchboard in the concrete barracks. The Northern Luzon Force began to operate from the old post headquarters that were now located on the second floor of Battery A Barracks, 24th Field Artillery.

Combat troops were now located in the field around the vicinity of the post. The newly organized battery of self-propelled mounts was in training out in the Bambam Trail area. These personnel were composed of a cadre from the field artillery units of the Philippine Division, truck drivers from the 200th, some Philippine Army soldiers and volunteer Filipinos who had been picked up off the highways. Trucks and private cars also were commandeered for the war effort.

Word came in that the Japanese had landed near Appari and Lanag. It was claimed that the Kelly bomb group had sunk some ships in the convoy. One battalion of the 12th Infantry opposed the landing at Appari for three hours, but because they had nothing heavier than machine guns they were forced to retire. Father Duffy figured the battery of the 11th Infantry gave some resistance at Lanag. This enabled the enemy to take over the airfield at Appari that was to have been dedicated on 8 December. Another field near Lanag gave them air bases. About the same time a landing was affected at Legaspi in the extreme south.

On Thursday, 11 December, a large group of Jap bombers struck again. Their mission was probably to hit the 26th Cavalry area. They succeeded in breaking the Signal Corps cable in the vicinity of Cavite headquarters and a couple bombs exploded in the end of headquarters B Troop but with little damage. Two more bombs exploded in the 2nd Marine Corps area and some duds went through the commissary and ice plant. About 30 duds were found in the cavalry corrals and a number over at the airfield. One bomb exploded and killed six men outright in the 200th Coast Artillery. Outside of those killed, the damage was negligible. The demolition squad's chief problem was removal of the duds.

It's believed that the low ceiling and cloudy conditions may have been responsible for the excessive number of duds. As a result of this attack, the headquarters of the Northern Luzon Force went to the field to take a position near cemetery No. 1.

The Manila area was being bombed every day about 12:30. Colonel Stanley L. James, who kept a daily account of their times of arrival, said that they were never more than 10 minutes off schedule for these noon-day bombings.

It was assumed that these planes were coming from a Taiwan base, but unfortunately, nothing could be done about it. The Jap air attacks had made United States air power virtually non-existent.

Clark Field came under attack again on the 12th and the officers quarters went up in smoke. However, no personnel were wounded. On the 11th, one of the Jap bombers had been shot down over the Zambele. The pilots had bailed out and were captured by the Balugas, who despised them for everything. They brought them into headquarters in the same manner that they carried their pigs to market -- on a bamboo rig.

"They were very scared yellow hombres," Father Duffy

said. "We untied their hands and tried to get some information out of them, then turned them over to the Military Police and sent them to Manila for questioning.

"We could not obtain any information about what stand we should take," he continued. "Higher headquarters was evidently awaiting developments, but General Wainwright was anxious to take the field."

Father Duffy spent the next days visiting various units of the tank, anti-aircraft and self-propelled units that had no Catholic chaplain attached to them. He heard confessions most of the days and parts of the evenings and had mass for the various units each day.

"On Sunday, I had a mass in the 2nd Battalion, 24th Motor Park for the 200th Coast Artillery men in that area, a second one in the battery A's mess and a third one at the hospital," Father Duffy said. "Authorization had been extended and Pullmans requested to evacuate the wounded from the station hospital to Manila."

On Sunday, General Wainwright decided to move his headquarters to the Bamban Hotel on Route 3. "This place was well-covered with shrubbery and a good choice for headquarters," he continued. "On the 14th Colonel O'Connor decided to get out of the post and moved his headquarters up in the vicinity of the 24th, 2nd Battalion Motor Park.

"Then on the about the 15th or 16th while visiting General Wainwright's headquarters at Bamban, I discovered five dead Japs that General Brougher had sent back from an encounter that one of his regiments had in the vicinity Vigas. We had to bury them in the compound near the hotel."

It was their first opportunity to see what the quality of Jap equipment was like. Their steel helmet was very thin, but they had a rather clever net that went over it for camouflage purposes. The gas mask also was cheaply made, the leather had "Made in the U.S." stamped on it. Their water bottles hung on a strap slung over the shoulder and held about a pint of water. Their mess kits were like the old-fashioned dinner pails of the '90s', the bottom of which was packed with steamed rice and the upper tray filled with a substance which tasted like chocolate fudge.

"On the visit," Father Duffy said "I was told by Colonel Nelson that General Wainwright had requested my assignment to Northern Luzon Forces from MacArthur's Headquarters. Then that night, Captain Herrick returned to the post and wanted to ship all our equipment and trunks to Manila to be stored and for safekeeping. I had some furniture that had been crated and sealed and waiting to be shipped on the 12th.

"Herrick took all that and together with trunks of mine, put it on a truck bound for Manila," he said.

"Outside of the daily bombings at Manila, there wasn't much going on of a military nature," he said.

Manila is capital of the Philippines and the principal port and trade center. It has a population of over a quarter of a million, and an area of 14 square miles. Manila Bay is one of the largest land-locked harbors in the world, 120 miles in circumference. The entrance to the city from the sea lies along the narrow channel of the bay, which is obstructed by the fortified island of Corregidor.

"Colonels Cook and Ray of the field artillery were having dinner with me nearly every evening and Mesario fixed us a couple of good rib roasts," Father Duffy said. "We ate early because of the blackout and it was almost imperative for Mesario to be off the post before dark On evenings when this could not be affected I always took him to the Sapang Bato Bridge because sentries stopped us about every one hundred feet.

"Colonel Donovan, who was up in a liaison mission from Manila, dined with me one evening and Ray generally stayed with me at night except when he was the night Officer of the Day at headquarters."

On the 19th, Father Duffy received orders to join General Wainwright's Northern Luzon Force. "Then I arranged to get a trunk to take the remainder of Herrick's and my things to Manila the next day," Father Duffy said. "Colonel Cook went with me to Colonel James' quarters where we stored the trunks and baggage and furniture crated for shipment. The furniture and household equipment was stored in Colonel Cook's field artillery cement quarters.

"We put the crates in Colonel James' lower servant's quarters and the suitcases upstairs off of his back porch. Immediately after this had been completed, Manila came under an air raid by the Japs. They struck Cavite and Nichols Field.

"We went into the yard during the raid near some slit trenches, but didn't need to use them since the action was some distance away," he said.

After the all clear, they went to the Army-Navy Club where they met General King and Colonel Williams. General King had received his promotion to major general, so they had lunch and discussed the general situation and the imminent fall of Hong Kong.

Afterwards, they went to pick up Colonel Cook, who had been storing records in town. Then they returned to the post and arrived about 5 in the evening. Mesario had prepared a fine meal for them and had everything ready for Father Duffy's departure to the field.

After dinner, Father Duffy went to Colonel Pierce's quarters where he spent some time with him, O'Connor, Major Daley and Rosy O'Donnell.

The next day, Sunday, the 23rd, Father Duffy celebrated mass for the 200th, the post and the hospital. He turned over the chaplains' fund to Chaplain Ralph Brown and the rest of the post funds that were under his custodianship.

After loading equipment in the car with Mesario's help, Father Duffy left for the northern front.

"I would have liked to have taken Mesario with me, but he had his sister to take care of," Father Duffy said. "So I gave him some money and told him, 'I want you to return to me when we can again be on the post.'"

Father Duffy arranged for Mesario to work for Colonel Ray, but the houseboy remained long enough to wash Father Duffy's soiled clothes and sent them to him. Mesario then left Colonel Ray to take his sister somewhere in the vicinity of Santa Rita-Cabanatuan to protect them in the coming assault.

Upon Father Duffy's arrival at Northern Luzon Forces quarters stationed along the Agno River about six kilometers west of Vilasese, General Wainwright extended him a warm welcome to his command and instructed his aide to find a place to locate the car. The general assigned the major to the same tent occupied by Colonel Nelson.

Components of the general's 11th Division had been contacting and carrying on patrol fights with advance elements of the Japanese along the Lingayen Gulf corridor north of San Fernando, La Union.

This activity was a little disturbing to the general, so he decided to wipe them out the next morning and issued an order to attack against those forces.

"We were sitting around after supper speculating whether it was a mistake to wipe them out. This force might be trying to draw us north in the event that the Japs wished to strike at Lingayen." Father Duffy said.

However, the order had been issued, but the general was a little uneasy about it. About 7 p.m. a message came from general headquarters in Manila that stated an American submarine had sighted a large Japanese convoy, well escorted by cruisers and destroyers about 110 miles north of Lingayen, traveling at about nine knots an hour. Estimated strength of the convoy was about 95 vessels, estimated time of arrival in the vicinity of Lingayen about 8 a.m. the next morning.

It was necessary to immediately annul all existing orders and order all division commanders to report at once to Northern Luzon Force command post with the least possible delay. A battalion of the 86th infantry with a battery and stationed at Calisse, San Jacinto, and Lingayen were alerted and told to expect a landing threat between 4 and 5 o'clock the next morning or before.

Plans for disposition of forces were being made while division commanders were en route to headquarters. The situation was critical and serious.

"We had no air power that we could use against the Japs and they had complete superiority of the skies," Father Duffy said. "We had no experienced troops except the one battalion of the 86th and 26th Cavalry. The 11th and 21st Infantry of the 11th and 21st Divisions were the only troops that had received a month's training. The 12th and 22nd had been organized on 6 December and the 13th and 23rd had been together only two days.

"The 21ast and 11th Field Artillery had never fired a gun; the 71st Division was at O'Donnell, the 91st at Cabanatuan and the 31st along the Zambales Coast," he continued. "The 91st and 71st were not released to us even at this time.

"In addition," he said, "we had one battalion of tanks and an improvised battalion of self propelled mounts. It was a pathetic picture. General Wainwright dictated the disposition of the 11th assigned to Lingayen Bay between Dagupan and San Fernando, La Union, and the 21st was to cover Lingayen and the Obando Bay side with protection and probably withdrawals down Highway 13.

"It was requested that the Navy be ordered to attack the approaching convoy," he said. "Requests were made for air power to attack at dawn, but such was not available except for two on those ships.

"Orders were issued to do everything possible to prevent the landing," Father Duffy continued. "I was disgusted with General Brougher that night when he affirmed that, 'This is the end of a glorious military career.' Brougher had never impressed me favorably although I had noted in the previous January maneuvers that General King thought quite a bit of him. He'd always impressed me as one of our self-propagandized, ambitious officers who was full of canine excrement and had little on the ball. His sending of five dead Japs to Luzon Force headquarters to prove he had killed four of them was further evidence that he was preparing for some Rotarian talk and he wanted to prove this point beyond question as far as I was concerned. The next morning in the vicinity of Bauang, he was giving his officers a pep talk. He told them they were to fight to the last man and not run, and when the dive bombers came over, he left them all standing out in the open while he dashed as fast as his legs could carry him to a fox hole."

The Japs sailed in on schedule. The 155's waited until they were within range, then opened up on them. The Japs lost a few boats, but they pulled up, moved out of range of the 155's 'and landed almost unopposed at Damortis and in the vicinity of San Fernando.

Captain Jones' battery of self-propelled mounts distinguished themselves that day on Baguio Road in the vicinity of Bauang until the Japs were 200 yards in front of them. They were forced to withdraw up Baguio Road, but pulled out with their guns blazing. Some other elements of the 11th also evacuated that direction.

When Jones arrived at Baguio, he wanted to proceed down the Megellan Trail and could have gotten his battery through, but the colonel wouldn't let him. They were forced to abandon their guns and trekked down Highway 5 of the Cagayen Road where they commandeered trucks and got back to American lines about seven days later.

Organized and systematic dive bombing that produced a terrorizing effect on the inexperienced Filipino troops covered the enemy landing operation. On 22 December, the Vilarsese Bridge was bombed, the south span was damaged, and the 12th Infantry was in retreat.

Chapter VII

The Surrender of Bataan

On the morning of 23 December, the 71st Division – minus the 71st Infantry – had moved into position along Route 3 south of Sison. The 72nd Infantry and 71st Engineers were in the front lines with the 71st Field Artillery in support to the rear. The 26th Cavalry, which had suffered heavy losses, received orders to fall back through the 71st Division line to Pozorrubio to reorganize. The 91st Division, USAFFE reserve at Cabanatuan, had been attached to the North Luzon Force and its 91st Combat Team was ordered north to reinforce the 71st Division.

With the situation growing grimmer by the hour, American commanders hastily called a meeting to set up lines of defense and withdrawal. That night, the Japanese launched an attack and drove the 91st Combat Team out of Pozorrubio, and that ended any hope of holding a line there.

By Christmas Eve, the Japanese had secured their initial objectives and established a strong foothold on northern Luzon. They were already in position to head south to Manila along Luzon's broad highways.

The Japs had taken Guam in two days, Wake Island in two weeks despite heavy resistance from U.S. Naval and Marine forces. Japan had practically destroyed the U.S. Navy's Pacific Fleet in the attack at Pearl and now controlled the air around the Philippines.

American and Filipino troops on Bataan were backed by those on Corregidor where MacArthur had established the U.S. Far East

Command Headquarters. In the Malinta Tunnel there were about 5,000 men, sixty-eight women (nurses, civilian and army wives) and children, including MacArthur's four-year-old son, Arthur.

Bataan and Corregidor were to support each other. They would either both survive, or both fall. The Japs attacked Bataan first.

The first line of defense, the Abucay-Mauban line, on Bataan fell on 22 January 1942. Generals Wainwright and Parker's troops were separated by Mount Natib, were outnumbered and retreated to the second and final battle line, the Bagac-Orion Line. Two days later, MacArthur knew Bataan would fall.

He ordered food stocks on Bataan to Corregidor with hope that reinforcements from the U.S. would arrive by July. If Bataan fell, the Philippine Division would be transferred to Corregidor. But troops were not transferred. They held the line and both sides would continue to fight with heavy casualties, and Japan couldn't break through.

By 8 February, General Masaharu Homma, commander of Japan's 14th Army, was in big trouble. His losses were so great in dead, wounded and seriously ill that he was forced to end his offensive and retreat. By 24 February when his withdrawal was complete, his 6th Division had gone from 14,000 troops to 712. Nara's 65th Brigade to 1,000 men from 6,500 and many of those were ill and weak. Homma's strength had gone from regiments to companies.

Homma finally received reinforcements on 24 March, but by then MacArthur had been ordered to Australia and Wainwright assumed command of the Philippine forces.

Bataan's defenders believed, and MacArthur supported their beliefs, when he told them help was on the way in the form of thousands of troops and hundreds of planes. He also told them there were plenty of supplies.

However, those who knew that Japan controlled the Pacific were aware that convoys could not come and they were silent about it.

MacArthur transferred a thousand of the ten thousand tons of food from an Army depot in Cebu to Bataan, but that would last for only four days. By March, attempts to run blockades from Manila were too dangerous.

With the Bataan situation very serious, soldiers tried to divert their attention to other more enjoyable moments, so pilots down at Mariveles threw a party in early March. To pass the time between battles, soldiers played volleyball and in the hospital, chaplains put on entertainment nights for patients. Usually, though, chaplains were doing ministerial duties.

The Japanese bombed the two hospitals that were suppposed to be safe on Bataan. The first time was an accident, and they apologized, but later, the bombings became intentional despite a visible Red Cross. That action violated the 1929 Geneva Convention.

Food and medical supplies were so low that soldiers began to eat anything. They were down to two meals a day and even less, drinking from dirty streams when clean drinking water was not available. Combined with contaminated food, this caused deadly medical conditions. Medical units, besides treating the wounded, were running makeshift operating rooms and other wards in addition to dealing with various illnesses. They lacked proper medication in many cases and particularly quinine. Nurses had to sterilize used dressings and re-used them. It became more obvious that the Bataan defenders couldn't hold on much longer with Japanese attacks becoming more intense.

By 3 April 1942, General Homma, with fresh troops, launched a full-scale attack on Bataan. But the next day, 4 April, while Homma's troops were having their way on Luzon, the USS Hornet, one of the Navy's newest aircraft carriers, sailed out of San Francisco with a rare cargo – 16 Army Air Corps B-25 medium bombers. The Hornet's sister ship, the USS Enterprise, had sailed six days earlier. They were the key ships in Task Force 16.

No one had any idea where TF 16 was headed. Rumors circulated that they were taking the B-25s to a base in the Aleutian Islands, or perhaps to a Russian air field on the Kamchatka Peninsula. That seemed reasonable. B-25s obviously were too big to take off from an aircraft carrier.

Then on 7 April, over sixty nurses on Bataan were evacuated to Corregidor. Some would make it to Australia before that stronghold finally fell. Some of them, however, were never seen again.

MacArthur's orders to Wainwright were that he was opposed to any circumstances or conditions to the ultimate capitulation of this command. He also ordered Wainwright to attack if food failed. President Roosevelt agreed and issued a "no surrender" order which was forwarded by Wainwright to General King on 4 April.

Americans and Filipinos were faltering due to poor health, and General King concluded that he had no alternative but to surrender. On 8 April, they could no longer fight.

Father Duffy, now the First Philippine Corps chaplain under General Wainwright, had been involved in the battles at the Moron-Begac breakthrough on 18-19 January and Agaloma Point from 22 January to 4 February 1942.

The final breakthrough that forced the surrender of the Bataan defenders came between 4-8 April when Japanese troops overran the 2nd Corps. Some units of the 1st Corps and remnants of the 2nd Corps collapsed and straggled to the rear lines. Then about 2 in the morning of 9 April nature even stepped into the picture when a severe earthquake rolled across the Bataan Peninsula and over to the island of Corregidor. It shook Bataan like a leaf and collapsed some barracks, and was so severe that some thought it might be the end of the world.

A few hours later, the ground began to shake again almost like another earthquake, but soldiers learned that the ground shaking was due to explosions from the destruction of remaining U.S. ammunition dumps and supplies so they wouldn't fall into enemy hands.

About 10 in the morning, General King, who was an Atlanta, Georgia native and grandson and nephew of Confederate officers who had fought during the Civil War, surrendered some 79,500 American and Filipino troops to Jap commanders General Homma and Major General Kameichiro Nagano. It was the largest U.S. military force to ever surrender in the history of the United States.

From his post on the island of Corregidor, General Wainwright sent a message to General MacArthur after learning

74

about King's action,:

"General King, commanding Luzon Force, without my knowledge or approval, sent a flag of truce to the Japanese commander . . . Enemy on the east had enveloped both flanks . . . Physical exhaustion and sickness due to a long period of insufficient food is the real cause of this terrible disaster."

What contributed to the terrible conditions and death that followed was the fact that General Homma and his staff had estimated that the number of prisoners would be approximately 20,000. They didn't know such a huge number of prisoners would be involved in the surrender.

It took several days for all the Bataan defenders to get word of the surrender. On 10 April down south near Mariveles, Father Duffy's group received official word at General Wainwright's Command Headquarters of capitulation. There at Command Headquarters at the lower end of Bataan is where Jap forces captured Father Duffy.

Back on 8 April, the day before American and Filipino troops surrendered, the Enterprise, escorted by the cruisers Salt Lake City and Northampton, four destroyers and a tanker, sailed quietly out of Pearl Harbor, set a northwesterly course and headed toward the north Pacific. She was headed for a spot that would take her far north of Midway and stop on the International Dateline.

Chapter VIII

The Death March

The six-day, 80-mile death march actually began on 11 April and headed toward Camp O'Donnell. On the first day Father Duffy was confronted by Chaplain Robert Taylor*, a Southern Baptist minister from Texas. Father Duffy, a fairly short man and kind of scruffy looking, was barefoot, his trousers were badly torn, his knapsack covered with mud and he had a matted heavy black beard.

Taylor looked at Father Duffy. "If your bishop could see you now Duff, he'd excommunicate you."

"I'm not communicatin' anyway," Father Duffy said and forced a little smile. "If he saw me now, he'd vomit, I stink so bad."

They stood together laughing until one of the Jap guards came running toward them and shouted, "You no laugh! You no laugh!"

Later, Chaplain Taylor, who had been with the 31st Infantry throughout the Bataan Campaign, talked about the surrender.

"It wasn't so much hearing about the surrender as it was seeing the white flag go up, which is the symbol of surrender. I guess around 8 or 9 o'clock in the morning, the surrender flags went up. We got the word that General King had been ordered to surrender and that he had sent his contact people forward to confer with the Japanese to affect the surrender. This was a rather bad moment in the lives of most of us. You just can't imagine what the feeling is

77

unless you've been there to see the white flag being hoisted and the American flag being lowered in defeat. This is something we had never witnessed and never experienced. We were not prepared for it at all . . . no."

Aboard the Hornet on 13 April, rumors were put to rest by Vice Admiral William F. (Bull) Halsey. He signaled TF 16, now composed of two carriers, four cruisers and eight destroyers, supported by two tankers and a pair of submarines, was "bound for Tokyo."

Until that moment, none of TF-16's 10,000 men had any idea that they were part of such a daring mission. But President Roosevelt was determined to exact revenge for the attack on Pearl Harbor on 7 December. His military leaders had to find a way. The B-25s were it.

The first break in development of a plan came in early January 1942 when Captain Francis Lowe, from Admiral Ernest King's staff in Washington D.C., visited Norfolk, Virginia to inspect the new USS Hornet (CV-8). At an airfield close by, he saw the outline of a carrier deck painted on it and an inspiration occurred. Lowe began to research the possibility of ground-based bombers taking off from a carrier deck, big planes with longer range than a carrier-based bomber.

By mid-January, Captain Donald Duncan, Lowe's air operations officer, proposed that the Army B-25, with a ton of bombs and able to cover 2000 miles with additional fuel tanks, could launch off a carrier deck's short distance, bomb Japanese cities and fly to friendly airstrips in China.

Duncan and the Hornet's commanding officer, Captain Marc Mitscher, proved in February that a B-25 could take off in the 500-feet available on the carrier deck. Thus at a South Carolina air base, training began for the special launch.

Five days into the death march, on 16 April near Hermosa, Father Duffy passed out and fell by the wayside where he was bayoneted the first time. He was unconscious for a little while and eventually was befriended by a Japanese guard. When Father Duffy came to, the guard talked with him, gave him some tea to drink and then told him, "You better catch up with the other prisoners before another guard finds you. He might not be as friendly."

The next day, on 17 April, the Hornet, TF-16's flagship Enterprise, and four cruisers left the destroyers and tankers behind and made a fast run toward Japan. But before they could come into the planned 300-mile range, at 0300 on the morning of the 18th, Enterprise radar picked up two enemy contacts ten miles away from the task force, and at 0600, one of its planes flew low over the flight decked, dropped a weighted message that reported a Jap picket ship was 42 miles ahead and that probably the scout plane had been spotted.

At 0738, Hornet lookouts saw the masts of another Japanese picket ship while the carrier message center picked up broadcasts that TF-16 had been spotted. So Doolittle received an order for an immediate launch from Halsey and the Hornet swung into the wind, a 40-knot gale that brought seas to 30-foot crests, and heavy swells. Waves broke over the Hornet's bow, soaked deck crews and wet the flight deck. Colonel Doolittle's B-25 was the first to go and he had only 467 feet to get airborne. He managed to pull the heavy bomber into the air. By 0920, all 16 aircraft were airborne and en route to Tokyo, Kobe, Osaka and Nagoya. It would be the first strike against the Japanese homeland.

Doolittle's bomber departed three hours ahead of the others. It would still be dark when he arrived over Tokyo and they would drop incendiary bombs to light up military and industrial targets. The group would fly southwest afterwards, across the Yellow Sea and 600 miles into China to Chuchow and land at a friendly airfield with about 20 more minutes of fuel.

When news of the raid reached the United States and President Roosevelt was asked about the origin of the raid, his only reply was, "Shangri-La."

As the death march continued, on 22 April between Guagua and Bacalod, Pampanga along Highway 7, Father Duffy was bayoneted again, only this time, the Japs left him for dead. A group of soldiers witnessed the third bayoneting of the Catholic chaplain.

Some time before, he had fallen unconscious by the roadside and soldiers who saw him were certain he had died.

Two days before this incident, Father Thomas Scecina* had anointed him. They had left him beside the road to die, but he revived sometime during the night and caught up with the group of prisoners.

Father Scecina, like Father Duffy, came from Indiana, was born in Linton on 16 September 1919 to Slovakian immigrant parents from Eastern Czechoslovakia, George and Anna Scecina. And, like Father Duffy, he had been educated in a Catholic elementary school, St. Peter's at Linton, and attended high school and college at St. Meinrad Minor Seminary and School of Theology at St. Meinrad, Indiana from 1921-1935. He was ordained to the priesthood by the Most Reverend Joseph E. Ritter, Bishop of Indianapolis, at the Cathedral of Sts. Peter and Paul on 11 June 1935.

Father Scecina also studied at Catholic University in Washington, D.C. during 1936 and earned a Bachelor of Arts Degree in Cannon Law, returned to Indianapolis in 1938 and worked as an assistant at St. John's Church. The following year, he founded the Catholic Information Bureau for the diocese.

Father Scecina was commissioned a chaplain in the U.S. Army in 1940 and reported for active duty at Fort Harrison, Indiana. He was assigned to Camp Polk, Louisiana and from there, was ordered to the Philippines.

Chaplain Albert Braun told Father Scecina that just prior to this last Father Duffy incident, a Medical Corps captain had given Father Duffy a shot of morphine to ease him into eternity. He was certain Father Duffy was dead, that apparently the Japanese soldier, after he slashed Father Duffy's foot with his bayonet and he didn't move, was satisfied also that he was dead. Father Braun believed that's why the soldier didn't bayonet Father Duffy in the stomach.

Information about Chaplain Taylor and Father Thomas Scecina is printed from the book Brothers of Paul written by Richard S. Roper, published by Revere Printing, Odenton, MD, 20 April 2003.

Top: A Japanese guard wipes his bayonet after killing a POW that collapsed as the Bataan Death March begins.

Bottom: The captives are only fed twice on the entire Death March. Philippine citizens throw food from the side of the road and prisoners must fight for it.

(Drawings by Sgt. Ben Steele. U.S. Army Air Corps)

After all the prisoners and Jap guards had passed by him, two Filipino guerillas emerged from the underbrush near the side of the road. They found Father Duffy and immediately checked him.

"He's still alive," one guerilla said.

"Okay . . . let's get him away from the road and out of sight before any Japs come back," the other one said.

So they quickly carried him from the side of the road into the brush and away from the area in case any other enemy soldiers returned for they knew if the Japanese found him they'd kill him.

A little while later, Father Duffy regained consciousness and the Guerillas began to feed him, care for him and then transported him to a shack back near the fishponds. That's where Father Duffy discovered eight other American soldiers who also had been on the death march and rescued by the Guerillas.

They remained there at the shack for about a week, but five of the Americans were so ill and feeble that they died during that time. Father Duffy had begun to regain some strength and helped bury them there in the fishponds so the Japs wouldn't find them.

Father Duffy's blood poisoning from the bayonet wound became so bad that he couldn't walk. Finally on 3 May, his acquaintance, Bernia, arranged for him to be moved by Calesa. Fearlessly and under cover of darkness, the Guerillas carried him straight down the main highway to the Convent of the Dominican Sisters at Guagua where the Santa Familias Hospital was located.

Father Duffy remained hidden in their infirmary for four months. Despite the foot wound, he directed guerilla activities and information services in five provinces of Luzon – Bulacan, Pampanga, Zambales, Tarlac and Bataan -- from his hospital bed. Four times Japanese guards searched throughout the hospital for him, but failed in their quest.

He worked under the direction of Colonel Claude Thorpe, General MacArthur's guerilla chief, but because of the Japanese searches of the hospital and his fear that his presence might endanger the Sisters, he left before his infection was cured.

The death march for some lasted about six days, but for others it was twelve. A report estimated that 5,200 Americans died on the march, but the dying went on at Camp O'Donnell, and the death count went to a high of about 550 men a day.

During the next six months in which Father Duffy directed Guerilla action, he also lived with the Guerillas, forces that were composed of American stragglers, Hucks, Nigritos, Chinese and Filo-Americans.

Father Duffy's foot became infected again, so he soaked it in an Epson Salts solution for six weeks and cured it. When he finally was rid of the infection, he went out to participate in the Guerillas capture of a Japanese battery at Saxamonan, when they turned the guns on the Japanese and fired until all the ammunition had been used up. While they were using the Jap cannon, he discovered an American flag in the caisson. That flag became very precious to him, so he took it when they abandoned the battery.

The American flag became a significant part of Father Duffy's life. He eventually wrapped it around his body and under his underwear to keep it hidden. Later, he would hide the --- securing a commission in 1920. Chaplain Wilcox, who had also served in World War I, would take it back to the United States and send it to Father Duffy's niece, who received it in June 1945 and flew Old Glory in the state of Ohio all the rest of the time he was a POW.

After his wounds healed, Father Duffy took off and spent several months going from one unit of Guerillas to another to give them a chance to attend Mass and receive the Sacraments.

In January 1943, Father Duffy was betrayed by a Filipino who wanted to kill another man who seemed to be in sympathy with the Japanese. The Filipino's assassination plot was discarded by Father Duffy because the intended victim, the chaplain knew, was a double agent and worked for the Americans. Thus the Filipino, who wasn't aware of the situation, turned Father Duffy in to the Japanese, where he was recaptured and taken to Fort Santiago.

In the next few days, the Japanese tried to gain information from Father Duffy by torturous means. One of his captors used a baseball bat to beat him, but the Major wouldn't talk. Then they gave

U.S. War Department and World War II: America at War 1941-1945 by Norman Polmar and Thomas B. Allen.

him the agonizing pressurized water treatment, but he still wouldn't talk. During the torture, Father Duffy expected to be killed and told them flatly, "Even if I knew anything I wouldn't tell you. I'm paid to die for my country, so cut out this foolishness and either chop my head off, like you've done with others, or shoot me."

For that remark, the Japanese interrogator gave him a slap in the face. A half-minute later, he gave Father Duffy a cigarette and a drink of scotch.

After this torture session, the Japs decided to put him on trial as a Filipino Guerilla in a Kemptai Court Martial. They brought in two spies to testify against Father Duffy, but somehow, he believes, with God's help he managed to overcome their testimony.

For his defense, Father Duffy testified that he didn't bear arms and he produced witnesses who verified this to be the case. He argued to the court that it wasn't his fault he was not with the forces when they surrendered, and also pointed out that it was the Japanese guards who left him for dead by the side of the road during the death march.

To Father Duffy's great surprise, the court acquitted him. He then was accepted as a Prisoner of War and became the only American officer to ever beat a Kemptai Court Martial.

The Japanese sent him on to the penitentiary at San Fernando for 10 days, then from Fort Santiago to the infamous penal institution Bilibid Prison at Manila. He arrived there in February 1943. After a few weeks, he obtained a Mass Kit and served as the Catholic Chaplain at Bilibid. Except for a work detail to Lipa in May and June that year, he remained at Bilibid until 13 December 1944.

All along the way, Father Duffy encountered other chaplains who performed far beyond their duties. Another such chaplain at Bilibid prison was First Lieutenant Carl Hausmann, who was born in Weisenberg in Alsace-Lorraine in France while his parents were visiting there. They returned to their home in Union Hill, NJ where he graduated from high school. He eventually studied Theology at Woodstock College in Maryland and did his Tertianship in 1932-33 at St. Andrew's in New York. In 1933, he became Procurator Socius to the Master of Novices at Novaliches on the Island of Luzon and assigned to the Colion Leper Colony on Mindanao. He was there when hostilities began and entered the Army.

Father Hausmann's Army career was about two days long. He became a prisoner of war immediately after the surrender. He eventually was sent to Cabanatuan in June 1944 where he said mass by candlelight in a rude chapel other chaplains had built. His reverence when he served at the altar impressed everyone, including other priests.

To indicate that Father Hausmann stood for Christianity, religion in general and for God, Catholics referred to him as St. Joseph. Non-Catholics called him the Holy Ghost and they didn't intend it in an irreverent way.

As Father Hausmann's body wasted away during his POW days, others could see there was something special, something deeply spiritual about him. This was apparent even to strangers.

One survivor who knew him only slightly said of him, "Maybe he was too much at home with God. He was so thoroughly in the state of grace that it made the rest of us feel unclean, uncomfortable. It's not natural for a man to give away his food when he's starving, to work for someone else when he himself can hardly stand up. Holiness is an easy thing to hate, and he was holy, but we liked him."

Father Duffy talked about the time in November 1944 when Father Hausmann defied his captors. In his bare feet and ragged clothes, he was saying Mass for a group of prisoners. Just as he was ready to consecrate his chalice, the air raid alarm sounded. The men who had been kneeling around him scattered.

"A guard barked at him, but he stood with his eyes on the Host and didn't move. The guard came up to the altar, barked again, then struck him with the butt of his rifle. Carl would not move. A seaman who saw the whole thing said that the guard flew into a sudden wild rage and began to club the priest, beat him with the butt of his gun for ten full minutes.

"The sailor's estimate of time in a crisis like that is probably not reliable," Father Duffy said. "A ten-minute beating with a gun butt should have killed him."

Other prisoners ran into the courtyard and the angry guard

left the altar to drive them back. When the guard had gone, Carl finished the Body and Blood, and then went back to his cell.

During his time at Bilibid, Father Duffy casually walked among the prisoners and talked to many of them. That's when he encountered *Ben Steele, an Air Force sergeant who had been attached to the 19th Bomb Group at Clark Field when the Japanese attacked Pearl Harbor.

Ben was born and raised at Roundup, Montana in 1917, and the son of ranchers. He spent his early life on a ranch where he learned to hunt and fish and ride horses with his dad. He graduated from high school in 1939 and the following year, enlisted in the Army Air Corps.

He had arrived at Clark Field late in 1941 and at their Thanksgiving dinner, his commanding officer served an ominous warning to the group, that they should enjoy it because it might be a long time before they have another one as good. A short time later, their CO's prediction came true.

Sgt. Steele was among ten men who had been fighting in the front lines when General King surrendered on 9 April. "I didn't know any of them," he said. "During the night of April 8th, we were all separated from our units, it was so chaotic and terrible."

Sgt. Steele was on an ammunition trail about five miles west of Mariveles when he and the group he had joined encountered a Japanese tank that day. All of them were forced to surrender. The tank commander turned them over to guards who were handling other POWs who had been captured down near Mariveles. Steele and the others thus became part of the 8,000 American troops and 40,000 Filipinos that would begin the death march off the Bataan Peninsula the next day. Father Duffy also was somewhere in that group.

At the time of Sgt. Steele's capture, he and his ten comrades had not eaten in three days and had been without water and rest.

They all suffered from what other POWs suffered from – exhaustion, lack of food and water, dysentery, beriberi, pneumonia, blood poisoning and malaria. Steele lost track of time. All he

Top: Prisoners kneel before a makeshift altar created by chaplains at Bilibid Prison.

Bottom: A prisoner catches a rat and is envied by his friend. The men joke about their Cabanatuan "beef".

(Drawings by Sgt. Ben Steele, U.S. Army Air Corps)

knew was that men were dying all around him from starvation, disease, heat and brutality from Japanese guards. Sgt. Steele was to the point that death seemed a much better way out. No one seemed to be afraid, but they all thought they would eventually be killed.

Guards forced the POWs to carry their heavy packs, so burdensome that prisoners would fall under the weight. Then the guards kicked them, prodded them with bayonets until they got up and continued on. They staggered along for about four miles, almost to Mariveles.

Rumors began to circulate that there were trucks waiting that would carry them on up to the camp, but most men doubted what they heard. There were trucks along the way, but none of them were used to carry prisoners.

For the six days they were on the march, they received only two cups of rice. Guards tormented the prisoners, had no mercy for them, and if prisoners stumbled and fell, they were either shot or bayoneted. This was happening all along the line of prisoners. They were forced to walk close together, and at the start of the march they walked all day, all night and all the following day with no food, water or rest.

They were finally treated to a meager cup of rice on the third day, but no water. Many prisoners drank from polluted pools of water along the road, and if the guards didn't catch them and shoot them, some died from the stagnant water they drank.

One of the men Ben had met struggled to walk beside him, he was so exhausted. He finally pleaded, "Please, help me . . . help me . . ."

Ben also was struggling, but he managed to take the soldier's arm, put it around his shoulder and put his other arm around the soldier's waist. But a guard came up behind him, jabbed him in the rear with his bayonet. He wounded Ben and it forced him to drop the soldier. Then the guard killed the soldier as he lay there on the ground.

Ben had no idea how far they had marched when they finally arrived at their first stop in the town of San Fernando. He figured they had gone sixty-five miles and about nine days without food. From there, his group would be shipped to O'Donnell by train. But they were herded so tightly into boxcars that they couldn't sit down. The temperature was over 100 degrees and the sun beat down on the metal cars. Some prisoners died where they stood from a lack of air. Regardless, the train would carry them on to Camp O'Donnell.

"We were all in shock and wondered where and when it would end or when we would die," Ben said. "We were always hungry. The situation seemed so impossible . . . here we were POWs . . . the war had just started . . . and we were losing."

While at Bilibid prison, Sgt. Steele was ill for a long time. "I used to sit there day after day. I thought I'd lose my damn mind," he said. "I wanted something to do, so I started drawing with anything I could find to draw with. I'd draw on walls. People around me said, 'Why don't you draw the guys? You know, there are no photographs taken of this stuff.'

"So I started drawing stuff around the camp and sketches of people and portraits as close as I could on scraps of paper. I wasn't very skillful," he said.

Sgt. Steele became a self-taught artist during his days at Bilibid and completed some seventy drawings of prison life.

When Steele was sent to Japan in 1944 to work in the coal mines, he entrusted his drawings to Father Duffy, who hid them away at the bottom of his mass kit.

Father Duffy told Ben that he intended to write a book after the war and wanted Ben to illustrate it for him.

Some information on Ben Steele came from the book Brothers of Paul by the Rev. Richard S. Roper and the book Ben Steele, Prisoner of War, a partial exhibit of drawings on display at Northcutt Gallery of Art, Eastern Montana College, Billings, and also from personal interviews with him.

From the Death March prisoners go to Camp O'Donnell. They are told by a Japanese officer and interpreter what they have to do to survive in the camp.

Approximately 2,300 Americans die at Camp O'Donnell the first six weeks. Guards force a soldier to dig his own grave and they bury him in it.

Conditions are so bad at Camp O'Donnell, prisoners voulenteer for work detail on Tayabas Road. Of the 325 men assigned to the project, only about 50 survive, making Tayabas Road the worst work detail in the Philippines.

The dead are placed in individual graves with their dogtags tied to crossed sticks used as markers.

(All Drawings by Sgt. Ben Steele, U.S. Army Air Corps)

Top: On December 15th, 1944 Aircraft from the USS Hornet again
attacked the Oryoku Maru as it was moving across Subic Bay toward
Olongapo Point. One bomb made a direct hit on the hatch of the aft
cargo killing about 250 POW's

Bottom: The Oryoku Maru before the bombing.

Chapter IX
Oryoku Maru, Enoura Maru Hell-ships

The fateful journey from Bilibid Prison at Manila to Moji, Japan began on 13 December 1944. Bilibid also had been the central hospital for Luzon and manned exclusively by Navy doctors who were POWs.

The prisoners had been awakened early that morning, had breakfast of rice and Gruel about 5 a.m., and were prepared to leave Bilibid for the Manila waterfront at 6 a.m. There were over 1,600 POWs.

That day Father Duffy stood in line for an hour. "Then we were sent back to our barracks," he said. "Apparently there was some doubt about whether the detail should sail or not. At 11 a.m., we were lined up again. This time we were marched to the Manila waterfront, and from there, we could see the damage and destruction done to the port area by Americans in their bombings of 21 September 1944 and the subsequent bombings."

It was a difficult march for the prisoners, who carried most of their personal items, what clothing they had and what food they had managed to scrape together.

"We were assembled on Pier 7 and stayed there until 6 p.m.," he said. "and then we were loaded on the Oryoku Maru."

The Oryoku Maru, an impressive looking 15,000-ton cargo-passenger luxury vessel that once traveled the Orient, had begun taking on Japanese civilians, women and children about 3 o'clock that afternoon. Three hours later, the POWs were brought on board.

Father Duffy's section was placed in the No. 2 hold, located directly under the bridge. Because of the crowded conditions, they had only sitting room for their group, so no one got much sleep during the night.

"We had what we considered a good meal that evening," he said, "a worm-like fish with good rice . . . much better chow than we had been getting at Bilibid."

Late that night, the Oryoku Maru sailed out through Manila Bay and headed up the West Coast of Luzon.

The next morning, they received the same menu for breakfast, but just as they finished chow, American dive bombers from the aircraft carrier USS Hornet swooped in on the ships again about 9 a.m. The Japs manned pom-pom guns and three-inch anti-aircraft guns up on deck, but the attack continued until about 4:30 that afternoon. All Father Duffy and his section knew was that they were under way, someplace in Subic Bay, just past Corregidor.

"The Japs were good enough gunners to keep the Americans from hitting us with a bomb," he said, "but we had lots of casualties from machine gun fire."

Father Duffy had a close call when a piece of shrapnel caved in his hat, "but it didn't even scratch my head." He also had been wounded from shrapnel, and Japanese women and children and convalescent Japs were slaughtered on the upper decks from the great strafing runs by the planes.

During the morning attack, Chaplain Taylor, who also was aboard the Oryoku Maru Hellship, was hit by hot shrapnel in the right arm and hip. At one point, he almost lost consciousness. He couldn't move because of his hip and couldn't use his thumb on the right hand. Someone heard Chaplain Taylor pray: "Lord, are we finished? Lord, let us go down or get us out of here, but let us not die like dogs."

During the night, some of the Navy doctors were sent topside to help with the wounded, and those who could be, were evacuated from the ship. About four o'clock on the morning of the 15th, an alert came down for prisoners to prepare to evacuate the ship. "Take no shoes or gear," the alert said.

The prisoners waited, but by dawn, nothing had happened. About 6:30 a.m., a detail of doctors were taken topside.

"I learned later that they were put in a rowboat and started towards shore," Father Duffy said. "About 7 a.m., American planes were back, but there were no Jap gunners on deck now. A bomb hit in the after hold and another in our No. 2 hold. The one in the aft hold killed about 200 Americans. The one in our hold killed only a couple . . . it went off before it hit our section. After that, we were ordered to abandon ship, and as we did, American planes were back to attack again."

The POWs rigged up some "V" signs, so when American planes, flying low over Subic Bay waters, passed over, they apparently recognized them and didn't drop anything. "They tipped their wings to us and flew on," he said.

The battered Oryoku Maru had sailed about a mile out from shore when it ran aground. Prisoners began to leap over the side to escape the bombing and strafing. Most of them who were able swam ashore. "We were just off Olongapo, an old naval dry dock station," Father Duffy said. "Some of us went through and searched the ship before swimming ashore . . . the cabins and salons were filled with Jap dead, mostly women and children machine-gunned the day before.

"After making the mile swim ashore, we were taken in hand by Jap Marines. We had little clothes left . . . mostly a G-string and an undershirt, but we were permitted to lie around on shore for most of the day."

Father Duffy had lost everything, his vestments, mass kit and the drawings of Sgt. Steele that had been hidden in the bottom of the kit.

As the prisoners came ashore, Jap guards* were waiting, rounded them up and led them over to an old tennis court fenced in by boards and chicken wire. There were about 1,300 prisoners and only one spigot of water, so they had to take turns drinking from it. They had lost about 300 men in the bomb run that day.

About noon, American planes returned, dropped a few more bombs into the center of the Oryoku Maru and she burst into flames. In a few minutes, Davey Jones claimed what was left.

During the next week, prisoners were given four meals

each. They consisted of two tablespoons of uncooked rice per meal. Towards the end of the week, those who were without clothes were issued denim slacks and coats.

Father Hausmann was aboard the ill-fated Oryoku Maru and able to swim ashore. He was there on the tennis court where the men were crammed together. The weather was dry and over 100 degrees during the day. One observer saw Father Hausmann kneel down on his knees to talk with God, to beg for rain. There wasn't a cloud in the sky, not a hint of any rain. In about thirty minutes, there came a nice downpour to briefly provide some temporary relief.

"We buried 19 men just outside the court in shell holes," Father Duffy said. "Now, if you should say you cannot feed and clothe, house and hospitalize 1400 or more men on a tennis court for a week, I would have to disagree with you. I have seen it done."

From Olongapo, the POWs were moved to San Fernando Pampanga by truck, half the prisoners going one day and the other half the next. At San Fernando, half of them were housed in the penitentiary and the other half in a theatre. Here they received two hot meals on two days, a mixture of rice and sweet potatoes (locally called camoties).

About twenty of the seriously injured were taken from Father Duffy's detail at San Fernando. "We thought they were going back to the hospital at Bilibid," he said. "Some of us were envious, but rumors had it they were taken out and shot. From the best information I can gather, that's what happened. None of them were ever heard from again, and they didn't appear at either Cabanatuan or Bilibid from the statements of those whom I knew were left there."

On the morning of 24 December 1944, without food, they were loaded into boxcars and shipped north. When they passed by Clark Field, they could hear an aerial battle in progress, and figured the only reason they were not bombed was that U.S. planes had more important targets to hit.

About 4 a.m. Christmas morning in 1944, they arrived at San

Information obtained from Peart's Journal, a Prisoner of War Odyssey prepared from notes by Chief Pharmacist's Mate Cecil Jesse Peart, U.S. Navy, and presented to the Hospital Corps Archives.

Fernando La Union, were unloaded and corralled into a field and remained there until dawn. None of them had shoes and they walked over gravel roads to the outskirts of town to a trade school. They were fed two meals that day, one three-quarters of a canteen cup each of the rice and sweet potato mixture. Then about 7 p.m. that night, they marched out again in the dark, barefooted, over gravel roads for about ten miles to the beach.

"We came up behind Jap soldiers who were lying on the beach, ready to mann machine guns. Here we were allowed to rest," Father Duffy said. "The sand made a good bed – we were used to concrete floors, steel decks and wooden floors. We never knew a bed from the time of incarceration (until liberation)."

They were awakened about 5 a.m. on 26 December and each given a rice ball to eat. They all figured there was another march in store for them, but that didn't happen.

"We spent the day on the beach," Father Duffy said "and were allowed in the bay for a bath, the only one we had had since leaving Bilibid and the only one the rest would have for a long time, and the most any of us would ever have."

Two lieutenant colonels died on the beach that day and were buried in the sand. One of them was an old friend of Father Duffy's who had served in the Philippines for almost twenty-five years – Lt. Colonel Edmunds.

At dusk, they received a water ration and two tablespoons of uncooked rice. They tried to get some sleep, but were awakened at 4 the next morning and lined up. They waited for three hours with no breakfast. Then at seven, they were marched to the other side of the isthmus where the Japs had just finished unloading two transports of Cavalry. They were loaded into dorys, a flat-bottomed boat, and transported to the two ships.

"About 1,150 were put on one transport and 236 of us on the second," Father Duffy said. "I was on the second along with Jack Gordon, one of the naval officers from Bilibid prison. It was mostly the Bilibid doctors, corpsmen, naval officers and a few army fliers and a couple of civilians. The larger ship was to feed their prisoners. Our group was to go without food except for the scraps that came from the Nips mess due to the fact that our rations were on the other ship. We were on this boat from December 27 until January 6, 1945. We got about four meals during that time, about a cup of rice for each meal and a water ration of about a half of a tea cup a day.

"We had good order," he said, "and only lost six from malnutrition. We were, of course, very hungry, but the morale of the men was superb under the conditions and we had perfect control. So much so that when a propeller was shot off our ship one night and depth bombs were unloaded from above, the few who got scared were quieted at once. They really were a wonderful gang of men."

When they reached Takao Bay on 6 January, they were unloaded at the dock and then loaded into dorys again and taken to the ship that had the rest of their detail aboard, the Enoura Maru.

"Apparently they were so anxious to get out of Lingayen Bay that they couldn't take time to put us all on one ship," Father Duffy said.

They were fed rice again and a soup that had meat in it along with some tasty Formosan vegetables. They received three meals a day on the seventh and eighth, and in the afternoon, were allowed up on deck to get some sun.

"We were able to look over the harbor and could see that the Americans had been doing a lot of effective bombing and our hopes and our morale were high," Father Duffy said. "When the time came to go back into the holds, 500 of us were ordered into the forward hold, which had been filled with ammunition they had not been able to unload in the Philippines and which had just been unloaded that day at Takao.

"When the 500 of us go into this hold, we had nothing but squatting room," he said. "We were fed soup and rice that night and the same diet again the next morning. Just as we finished chow, we heard airplane engines . . . then all hell broke loose."

Allied pilots dropped four bombs directly into the hold where Father Duffy and all the men had been directed. "It seemed like hot irons struck my head, neck, arms and legs," he said. "My companions, whom I had just been talking to, were all dead except Egress. He had a big chunk of his head gone but he was conscious."

Father Duffy was bleeding from the head, neck, arms and

legs, but when he got up, he realized he was in one piece. Then he began to give everyone general absolution.

"And the wounded started hollering for me," he said, so despite bleeding profusely, he went to work. "I thought it was the end and wanted to do all I could before the end came. The naval doctors followed, but we had a mess on our hands with over three hundred dead and most of the rest wounded."

Chaplain Taylor had been sent aboard the Enoura Maru also, and when the American planes attacked the ship, he recalled, "The Japanese rushed us back into the hold. This was a pretty terrifying experience to go through because you feel the impact of the explosion and then there's this falling debris and the flying planks and everything from the decks. Then there's the quiet moment when seemingly everything's over – complete silence. You don't hear a scream; you don't hear a moan; you don't hear anything for a moment. Then we began to get on our feet, because when something like this happens, you fall flat on your stomach and get as close as possible to whatever you're standing or lying on.

"I was kind of the leader of a group of ten men who were on the main deck receiving their rice and water," he said. "When the planes came, we just fell in a cluster right on deck. When I was able to get up, I had been wounded in my wrist and hip by flying fragments from shells or bombs. Only about two of us got up. The rest of them were all dead in my group. Those of us who were still alive began to do our best to help some that were wounded. There wasn't much we could do except to get around to them and see how badly they were hurt. It was a pretty terrifying thing."

Major Eckert, a Judge Advocate from Maumee, Ohio, was badly wounded (he would die a week later). Father Frank McManus also was badly wounded at the same time and would die on 22 January when they were en route to Moji. Father Hausmann also was aboard and survived the attack in Takao Harbor, but he had become more seriously ill.

"I knew we had to make room so the wounded would be more comfortable," Father Duffy said, so he called for volunteers among those who were not wounded and the not so seriously wounded to help stack the dead on one side of the hold. Ensign Gordon was one of those who volunteered to move all the dead to one side of the ship. He was not seriously wounded, but had a couple of flesh cuts from bomb fragments.

Father Duffy was familiar with Ensign Gordon since he happened to know the Naval files a little better than the average Army person. He was the Catholic Chaplain at Bilibid Prison, which was the central prison hospital for Luzon and manned exclusively by Navy doctors. The entire staff of the old prison hospital was aboard the Enoura Maru, and as it turned out, Doctors Smith, Langdon and Father Duffy were the only survivors.

It seemed natural, then, that they should be in the section with naval personnel on that detail, which was composed chiefly of junior army field officers, civilians and naval personnel, mainly doctors and corpsmen.

After the dead were cleared and a place made where the legless and armless and the seriously wounded could be cared for, Jack Gordon was helpful in an attempt to comfort the wounded and feed them.

"Jack was a fine, outstanding man," Father Duffy declared. "I never knew his religion. It never mattered to me. In fact, I knew he believed in God and could care for his fellow man. We were all American and comrades. He was a real comrade to his fellow soldiers in one of our darkest hours."

After the attack, Father Duffy was able to administer the Sacraments to the dying and wounded and assisted in straightening out "the goriest mess I ever expect to see."

One of those Father Duffy administered the last Sacraments to on deck was Father Zerfas from the Diocese of Milwaukee. His leg had been blown off at the knee by one of the four bombs that landed in the hold where the 500 American prisoners had been quartered. Three hundred were killed outright, everyone was wounded and a hundred more died during the three days they remained in that hold with no food, water or medical care. Of the remaining hundred, most died before they reached Moji, Japan on 31 January 1945.

*Father Zerfas had been sent to the Philippines and to Father Duffy several months before the attack on Clark Field and assigned to the 26th Cavalry that had been almost wiped out at Sison in Northern Bataan. He had accompanied cavalry units on 70 missions behind enemy lines and singled out for gallantry in these actions.

In part, the decoration stated, "Chaplain Matthias Zerfas is herewith cited for bravery for having stayed exposed in the open in order to comfort a badly wounded soldier while other able-bodied men sought a much needed cave."

It was during that time that Father Zerfas encountered noted war correspondent Ernie Pyle, who described the Catholic chaplain as "a bearded priest from Wisconsin who wears a pith helmet and looks like Hailie Selassie."

Chaplain Zerfas had also survived the Death March and Camp O'Donnell and was sent to Cabanatuan. Chaplain John Curran described Father Zerfas' daily routine:

"He would get up and say Mass around 4:30 or 5 a.m. at an outdoor altar in the dysentery area. At 7 a.m., he'd begin delivering milk to the 600 patients; a cup of diluted canned milk to each man. He'd help those who were too weak to lift the cup. Some he fed by spoon. Dirt, filth and flies were beyond description. His milk route took three hours to finish. He'd then start around a second time, talk to the patients, cheer them up, and give them spiritual direction when needed. After a short timeout for his own lunch, which was on the starvation level, he'd be back with his patients, visiting them for another couple of hours. Then about 3 p.m. in the afternoon, he'd bring milk to the patients again. He always had a large convert class going and received a number of men into the church."

Not only was Father Zerfas steady emotionally, he was big and strong physically and spiritually. In a letter Chaplain Stanley Reilly wrote to Msgr. Joseph Springbot: "He (Father Zerfas) worked as a daily laborer along with the general lot. This had the profound influence of bringing the priesthood of Christ right into the crevices of men's daily experiences. We think this labor was an apostolate (like a mission of an apostle)." Chaplain Reilly added, "We met at evening to pray in common the Rosary and night prayers. It had to be public for there was no privacy. One of our padres knew the old

* *Information on Father Zerfas was obtained from the Brothers of Paul book written by Richard S. Roper.*

style Manual of Piety for Night Prayers by heart. These, we priests and other prisoners, learned by heart. It was an experience to hear the several hundred men speak out to God night after night. All the rest of the camp listened respectfully."

After Father Duffy had given Father Zerfas the last Sacraments, he wrote a letter to Archbishop Moses E. Kiley, and in it, he stated: "Father Matt had his left leg practically blown off at the knee. He was in great agony and shock. After administering the Sacraments to him, with the help of a couple of others, I moved him to a clearing where I covered him with rags we salvaged from the dead to try and warm him. He was chilled and shaking badly. Father Zerfas knew that he was going to die. He was ready to go. He told me he was ready and wanted to die – that he had seen all of this world and its degradation that he wanted and he asked me someday to look up his father if I should ever get back to the States and tell him he had died like a man. Father Zerfas died about dusk on the evening of January 11, 1945, and we had to put him over with the others. On the 13th, the dead were taken from this hold and buried in a common grave on the beaches of Takao Bay, Formosa. No chaplains were allowed to go ashore with him, but some of the detail who took care of the interment told me that the spire of the Catholic Church in Takao could be seen from the places where they laid them."

One year later on the anniversary of his death, his classmate, Father Joseph P. Kiefer, wrote in the Steubenville (Ohio) Register:

"Dear Father Matt: Were you here to look over my shoulder as you did in years gone by you would blush as you read what I am penning about you. You would brush aside this deserving bouquet with your customary ejaculation – 'Applesauce.' Somehow I feel you are with me tonight. From your newly found home in paradise you must know what I am writing. It is a poor encomium for such a grand priest and friend, but accepts it for the sake of the good old days. You know it comes from the depth of my heart. All during those bitter months of your imprisonment I prayed for you. Now I am happy that you, who shunned recognition in college and who refused citations for heroism in the Philippines, have been decorated with heaven's highest award – the unfading crown of martyrdom. Next Sunday, on the first anniversary of your death, I shall offer the Holy

Sacrifice of the Mass that we, your friends in the priesthood, may follow your short cut to heaven over the steep but certain pathway of humility, devotion and brotherly love!"

For three days the Japanese kept prisoners who were still alive down in the ship's hold and without medical care.

Finally, on 12 January, the ones who could walk were taken out of the hold. They had to leave the others. On the 13th the dead were taken ashore and buried in a common grave.

"That afternoon, we were transferred to another ship (the Brazil Maru)," Father Duffy said. "There were still over a thousand of us alive. Here, we were placed in bays, a section of the hold planked off, making a shelf large enough to hold twenty-five men and another twenty-five were on the deck underneath. We happened to be in the same section, or bay. We sailed from Takao on 14 January. Those of us who reached Moji arrived on 30 January."

The last phase of the trip from the Philippine Islands to Japan was the most costly in human lives even though they were not attacked by Allied planes between Takao and Moji.

"We left with almost 1100 still alive and arrived at Moji with less than 500, and another 250 died within two months after our arrival in Japan," Father Duffy said.

As the ship made its way through the China Sea, Father Hausmann, who also had survived the attack on the Enoura Maru, a brilliant linguist and a deeply spiritual priest, died from his illness.

One tale of his death is extremely vivid.

He died in the hold, half-naked, lying on the deck in the darkness and filth, among men who were too exhausted, too sick, too accustomed to death and too near death themselves to make any fuss over him. After he died, they stripped his body, gave what clothes he had to the living. Then they dragged his corpse into a patch of light underneath the hatchway. They left him there until there were six bodies. Then the boatswain, whose duty it was, tied a running bowline around the knees and a half hitch around the neck, looked up at the hatchway and called out, "All right, take it away."

His body bumped against the side of the hatch and slid along the deck and out of sight. Other POWs could hear the shuffle of feet and the jabber of Japanese voices as he was dragged across the deck and stacked near the railing with the rest of the American dead.

"Carl died partly because he gave his food away," Father Duffy said. "We were getting two spoonsful of rice every third day and he gave his away. The shame of it was that the men he gave it to weren't worthy of it. He gave it to the whiners, the weaklings. When they complained he'd lean over and dump his ration into their cup without a word. The real men wouldn't take it. They kept their mouths shut . . . like Carl.

"The bodies were normally cast over the side into the sea," he said. "It's not known for sure that this was the case with Chaplain Hausmann. Some believe that together with others, his body was cremated to provide fuel for the Brazil Maru as it slowly made its way toward Moji, Japan. All that remains of the earthly life of Father Carl Hausmann is his stole and rosary. These were found in the pocket of his ragged shorts after his death."

After the war, Father Duffy wrote a letter from Walter Reed General Hospital in Washington D.C.:

"Enclosed find the stole and rosary of Father Carl W. Hausmann, S.J., 1ST Lt., Chaplain, U.S. Army, who died January 20, 1945, aboard a Japanese POW ship enroute from Takao Bay, Formosa, to Moji, Kyushu, Japan, of starvation and exposure to the elements at the hands of his captors. He was buried at sea. He was a tremendous influence for good. His utter abandonment of self during the long years of servitude and incarceration brought the gift of faith to many that sat in darkness. Pagans, who neither knew nor accepted Christianity, not only admired him but saw in him everything Christianity had stood for down through the ages. He was an example of his great Captain and King, Christ Jesus. May he intercede for us before the throne of God? I think he had it all over the Irish Father Doyle of World War I.

"Eight priests and seven Protestant chaplains died on this trip. Chaplain Taylor, a Protestant, and myself, the most unworthy of nine priests, alone survived with some four hundred others out of 1,619. Why, we know not, but we suspect that even the Lord did not want us.

"You may be justly proud of Father Hausmann. He reflected great credit upon the Church and his Order and was ever a living example of those virtues that we must idealistically hope for in an Altar Christian (one who celebrates mass in a Christian church.). May he remember us! I know that the good Lord took a great liking to him."

They were now in northern waters, and all were very poorly clothed. Their diet in this phase of the trip was regular, but meager. Each prisoner received about eight tablespoons of water per day, and twice a day they received half a teacup of steamed rice.

"The men were all suffering from malnutrition, years of starvation, exposure, neglect and no medicines," he said. "The doctors' personnel supplies had been used up. I thought that Jack (Gordon) was getting along fairly well. He was conserving his strength, took things easy, spent most of his time in the bay reclining, but about a week before he died, he developed some dysentary.

"We had talked frequently and smoked the same cigarette," Father Duffy said. "Whenever someone in the bay produced a cigarette, it was passed round for all to get a puff and everyone was always solicitous that the man who owned it would have the last drag on it. I don't know whether you can appreciate the comradeship of the cigarette, but it bound us all together. There was no question of who you were or what you were. We were all buddies and sharing in the great good from one of our members.

"The best was almost not quite good enough for the rest who shared your trials and sufferings and the inhumanities of the enemy." Father Duffy paused a moment. "It may seem a little thing to Americans at home who are used to all the abundance our country has, but in the days of want, nothing is more precious than tobacco, and when that's shared with all your group, it brings a comradeship that has no parallel in human life. It's treating your neighbor as yourself. It's treating him as you want to be treated. and it's one of the great goods that comes from human suffering and want. Reduced to the least common denominator, you realize you need your brother, and he needs you, and those who do not realize this are swept away early in the game."

Ensign Gordon died early on the morning of 29 January some distance from Japan and buried at sea the day before the rest of the prisoners landed on the Island of Kyushu.

Later, Father Duffy wrote about Jack Gordon in a letter to Jack's brother, who had been a Navy flight surgeon from Guadalcanal to Saipan: "I didn't know him long. He spent most of his prison days at Cabanatuan, only I was never there, but during the days we were thrown together, I got to like him very much. He came through when it counted and I will always consider him as one of the great unselfish men who have crossed my pathway and I'm glad that I knew him and saw him at his best.

"You and your family have every reason to be proud of him. He served his country well. He willingly helped his fellow prisoners in their darkest hours and gave unselfishly of himself, reflecting great credit on his parents, his family and his country. May his memory live long and may the nation have many others who will imitate his virtue and his valor.

"As the senior officer who survived the bombing at Takao Bay, Taiwan, I recommended all those who participated in the relief of the wounded after the bombing there for an appropriate decoration," he said. "My recommendation had to be made to the Chief of Staff of the United States Army. Many were gone. The Army decided to give them all a Bronze Star, and as your brother was among the twenty that I recommended for a decoration, he received it from the source to which I had sent the recommendation."

At Moji, there were many Australian, Indian and British officers besides many Americans. The officers were given half rations, but the rest were forced to work in the mines or do some kind of metal work.

Ben Steele had been shipped out on a different Hell-ship from Father Duffy and landed at Omine Machi, Japan. He and the prisoners in his group were issued clothing for the first time in two years, and then sent to work twelve-hour shifts in coalmines around Omine Machi. The only break they received from the coalmines came about every tenth day when prisoners carried fertilizer and did other jobs.

As it turned out, Omine Machi was located seventy-five miles from Hiroshima, where the first Atomic Bomb was dropped on 6 August 1945.

Father Duffy and Chaplain Taylor, meanwhile, had been moved to the Brazil Maru to continue his journey to Moji. They arrived there on 29 January 1945.

* Moji is a major port and industrial center on the Shinonoseki Strait. Prisoners who could went topside. Japanese medical personnel boarded the ship and were horrified at what they found. They immediately left the ship and returned a short time later with food and clothing. Prisoners disrobed in the cold and for some that meant simply taking off a G-string or very thin under shorts. Then they were deloused and issued a suit of cotton underwear, wool pants and a blouse. There were no socks, but prisoners were given British issue shoes. Most important, however, men were given water, the first time since 13 January, and they were allowed to drink as much as they wanted.

It was bitterly cold when the POWs began to leave the ship at 0900 and they spent most of the day in a warehouse. Over and over they were counted until they were divided into four groups. One group of 110 men was those too sick to move on their own, so they were hospitalized at Moji Military Hospital.

** Chaplain Taylor and Father Duffy were the only two of all the chaplains who had begun this trip to have survived. Within thirty days, all but forty of the 110 men had died.

Chaplain Taylor wrote of the Moji Army Hospital:
"We were placed on grass mats and given blankets. There were no fires in the building and it was cold, inside and outside. Snow, sleet and ice were everywhere about the hospital area. The Japanese did nothing for the patients for several days. They did give us some rice each day with a small amount of vegetables and fish. Within eight days after being admitted to the hospital, 70 patients had died. I

*Information on the debarkation at Moji and what happened there is from the book Brothers of Paul by Richard S. Roper. ** Information on Chaplain Taylor obtained from the book Brothers of Paul by Rev. Richard S. Roper.*

pulled myself from a cold pallet on the floor each day and conducted the funeral ceremony for the dead.

"Each night before sleeping, I conducted devotional services for men of the two wards in the hospital. We had lost all of our New Testaments and Bibles, so we quoted in unison passages from the Scriptures. The moments we spent in devotion constituted the only bright moments of our experience in the Moji Hospital."

Father Duffy was in a group that moved by rail to Omuta Prison No. 17 at Fukioka, Japan on 30 January. That night at the mess hall, he passed out and became a hospital patient at Omuta.

* "As close as I was to death, I was kept alive by the Christian's fighting faith," he remarked. "I fought grimly every hour, praying to God to spare me and to give me strength. My prayers were answered for I became stronger. When I had recovered somewhat, the men used to carry me to the bedside of the dying. There were many deaths every day.

"I did what I could for each regardless of his faith, and a look of ineffable peace came to the face of many a tortured soul in that last bitter hour on earth," he said.

He would be a patient there until 24 April, but on 1 April, Easter Sunday, 1945, the first Mass ever said would be celebrated at Omuta. They stole some Dutch-Latin Missal Raisen wine and wete flower break (a mixture of flower and sugar), and Father Duffy attempted to hear confessions, but because of conditions, was unable to.

"Two men had to hold me up when I said that first mass,' he said. "After the service, I was so exhausted that I had to lie resting for hours."

He celebrated mass again on 8 April and 15 April, but he had no vestments available.

From April 24 to the 27th, Father Duffy was en route from Omuta to Mukden, Manchuria and on the 25th, spent that night in Seoul, Korea. When he arrived in Mukden, he immediately

* Taken from a newspaper article in the 27 July 1947 Cleveland Plain Dealer written by J. K. Schmidt and reprinted in the History of Our Lady of Lourdes Parish (1853-2003), New London, Ohio.

became a hospital patient.

"When we got to the Mukden camp, we were treated much better," Father Duffy said. "One Japanese doctor should get a medal from the U.S. government for the way he brought and procured medical supplies for us."

Top: Prisoners taken to Japan to work in the coal mines are issued their first new clothing in two and a half years.

Bottom: Prisoners load large rocks onto flatcars and then roll the cars to a fill and dump them.

(Drawings by Sgt. Ben Steele, U.S. Army Air Corps)

(Map of Manchuria, where Camp Mukden is located)

Chapter X
The Mukden Arrival

Major A.C. Tisdelle*, who had been a POW almost from the start, labeled Father Duffy as one of those soldiers who wouldn't die when he limped into Camp Mukden with 96 other Americans from Camp Cabanatuan. Chaplain Taylor also was in that group. They were part of the survivors of the bombing and strafing of the Hell-ships Oryoku Maru and the Enoura Maru that was sunk in Takao Harbor on 9 January 1945.

"Father Duffy was more dead than alive when he got to our camp," said Major Tisdelle, "but he insisted on saying mass as soon as he could stand on his feet. He had a few Red Cross raisins out of which he made wine, and our cooks made unleavened altar bread."

On the first Sunday in May (5 May), Father Duffy celebrated Mass, the first time they had such a service in Camp Mukden. The altar was set up on the second floor of the barracks. Guards were posted at the first floor doors, but only 30 men were allowed to attend since it was thought that many men could disperse readily if the Japs came through.

Joseph A. Petak* recalled the scene. The altar was a box placed on a table. His vestments were field vestments that Father Duffy had been allowed to keep, and he had a crucifix. The factory

* Joseph A. Petak's description of the first Mass at Camp Mukden is taken from the Brothers of Paul book, and Major Tisdelle's comments are from an article written by Carl Wiegman in the November 13, 1945 edition of the Chicago Daily Tribune.

workers managed to smuggle in some candles and there was the raisin-jack wine and bread. The altar was covered with a blanket and some towels, but despite the primitive accessories, the scene had a sense of sacredness, and the room was very quiet. The sun was just rising, rays pouring through the windows to cast a hallowed light into the room. Mass was short without any interruptions or alarms.

"The Japs would no doubt find some reason to stop the service when they found out," Petak said. "We still had some white rats among us, but I left the makeshift chapel feeling much better than I had imagined."

Father Duffy's experiences had not made him fearful of the Japs, Tisdelle said. "He bawled out the camp interpreter every time he saw him and told him the Japs ought to be ashamed of themselves. Even the Japs admired Father Duffy."

Father Duffy was among the first group of POWs released from Mukden, Manchuria on 24 August 1945. Their first stop was Sian, China where he sent a radiogram to Bishop Alter at Toledo to let him know that he was on his way back to the states.

Father Duffy finally arrived in Calcutta, India where he was admitted to General Hospital No. 142, and followed up his radiogram with a letter that went into greater detail.

"At last we are free and by God's mercy, alive," Father Duffy wrote. "All of us who have survived know that God has been very good and are most grateful although many has been the day in the past when death would have been a merciful end to temporal suffering.

"It is difficult to understand the wonderful and mysterious works of God, but He certainly looks after His own.

"I'm still among the infirm and am now expecting to return to the United States by air on the first plane out of here," he wrote. "Henceforth, Alcatraz will hold no terror for the survivors of Bataan and Corregidor.

"We thought that we would be flown directly to the States," he continued, "but things have not turned out that way. We were kept at the Kunming General Hospital for about two weeks and have now been in Calcutta for over a week. I know not how long we'll be here. I suspect that we're undergoing a fattening (up) process after the lean years of Nipponese incarceration.

"I'm in fair shape now, though my legs still bother me to some extent from the beriberi. This was the result of that infamous boat ride from Manila to Moji in which two out of seventeen Chaplains survived. Yours truly, by the grace of God, was among the two. The other was a Protestant chaplain, Robert Taylor, from Texas. We rode four boats on that trip."

Father Duffy went on to tell about the Hell-Ships and the bombing and strafing that took place shortly after his capture.

"On the fourth ship we had a procession of death. We lost over five hundred from starvation and estimate that about two hundred of the original draft of 1,619, mostly officers, survived. (The draft was mostly officers, and only about twenty percent of the survivors are officers).

"Upon arrival in Moji, I was sent to one of the camps and put in the hospital where I remained until shipped to Mukden the last of April (1945). I continued to be a hospital patient in the Manchurian Prison Camp. The chow was better at this camp and I began to pick up under the care of Dr. Oki, who was one decent Jap. When the generals and colonels whom I hadn't seen since the fall of Bataan arrived on May 20th, they didn't know me, but with the care I received there and the enjoyment of American food, which now abounds, I'm really coming around.

"I went through the Northern Luzon and Bataan campaigns as the 1st Corps Chaplain under General Wainwright until he relieved General MacArthur when he was elevated to the Supreme Allied Commander in the Far East. Then General Jones, who hails from Boston and who won his stars on the battlefield, became my commander. Few will appreciate the genius of these two men and what they accomplished with untrained men, no food, no medicine and little ammunition.

"I believe," Father Duffy declared "that the presence of General Wainwright, in the heat of every battle, did more to encourage the men and give them a will to fight, and was more responsible than any other single factor for the courageous stand that a handful of Americans and some untrained Filipinos made against the invading hordes of Bushidoists. There was not a man who felt in that campaign that Wainwright didn't feel the same personal loss as though he were his own son.

"I do not believe there was anyone any closer to the General than myself. There was hardly a night that we failed to spend an hour or two together, discussing the events of the day," he wrote, "and legion are the times that I have seen his eyes fill and the tears roll down his strong, manly face for the men lost in that day's battle. None of the mothers who lost their sons in Bataan sacrificed more than this great general who, against overwhelming odds, was offering each of his sacrificed soldiers as though they were his own flesh and blood upon the altar of defense, that liberty might live and that America might awake from her slumbers and realize that gangster nations can only be controlled by the presence of sufficient police power, to make them do right and shun the despoiling of the weak.

"Often he spoke of consecrating Bataan to the men who died there and raising a monument in their honor. His single wish was to dedicate himself and the days that God might yet give him to the memory of his boys who died and bled in repelling an unjust aggressor.

"I have not seen the general since he took command of the entire Philippine Theatre, but I know from others that he has been beaten and abused by his captors just as the rest of us were. We hope that the nation will appreciate this soldiers' general, known to us as Skinny, but as the quarterback because he was always in there calling the plays, and honor him fittingly because for those of us who survive as well as those who have paid the full measure of devotion, he was greater in the defeat that was ours than others could have been in victory."

Father Duffy went on to admit that he didn't do well on the death march. "In fact, I passed out a couple of times, was anointed once by Father Tom Scecina (whom I think was lost at sea with 1,800 other POWs), and on the 12th day without food, passed out completely, was bayoneted by a Nip guard and left for dead. That was in the vicinity of Betis Pampanga. I came to in the hands of a couple of Filipinos who had rescued me after the column passed."

He went on to tell about being recaptured and had expected

to be executed, but managed to beat the Kemptai court martial.

"You know that I've spent many years among the Filipinos and thought that I knew them. The Scout Division had been superb in battle," he wrote. "In fact, I'm sure that no outfit that fought under the Stars and Stripes surpassed them. It was only while moving from place to place with the irregulars that I learned their true greatness, their loyalty to America, their unselfish sacrifices, their passive resistance, their harassing resistance in the face of certain death, their constant fidelity, their daring in an attempt to bring aid to American POWs, though hundreds of their race had their heads lopped off by the invaders for their devotion to the Americans. Their valor and the unequaled bravery of their womanhood in the face of the most desperate odds should endear them forever to all Americans.

"They, as a people, never lost hope. They felt the shame and pain of the Americans' incarceration more than we did and whenever they met any of us, there was always a friendly "V" and the familiar salutation, 'It won't be long now.'

"No group under Old Glory had suffered more, none have been more loyal and I hope that we will consider the real desires of the average Filipino before we cast them adrift. The peoples of the East trust America. They look to her with hope. They want her to take world leadership. Probably the same is true in Europe," he continued. "But the East does not trust the nations of Europe. Neither do they trust some of their own leaders.

"Only the other day in China a distinguished citizen of that country expressed the hope that America would remain and help in the establishment of a stabilized government. And I hope that in regard to Japan that we have vision enough, that after the perpetrators of evil have been punished, we will be able to take advantage of the task before us and bring them out of the darkness of paganism through enlightenment and Christian teaching. It is my opinion that through the humiliation of defeat they may be able to learn to follow the true Son of God and I hope that the church in America is able and ready to play her part in the role of spiritual rehabilitation of these misguided people."

Father Duffy told the Bishop that as soon as possible after his arrival stateside, he would apply for leave. "Then you may expect me out Toledo way," he said. "There were several from Toledo and many from your diocese in the fallen Philippine forces. Some have made the supreme sacrifice. Eternal rest be theirs. Port Clinton was probably hit the hardest. General Weaver hails from Fremont and headed the Tank battalions and is on his way home. He was always very interested in his Ohio boys.

"God took a great liking to most of our gang and those of us who survived," he wrote "and dedicated ourselves to our comrades who gave all . . . that we might live."

While Father Duffy recuperated in a military hospital near Washington D.C. during 1946, military tribunals began hearing cases in Yokohama, Japan. Defendants included Shinto priests, medical personnel, professors and farmers along with military personnel of all ranks. Most trials involved maltreatment, beatings, starvation and general neglect that caused the deaths of thousands of prisoners of war.

One of those trials centered on Lieutenant General Matsaharu Homma, the 14th Army commander and the man responsible for the Bataan Death March. He also was responsible for the bombing of the city of Manila after it was declared an "open city" by General MacArthur.

Evidence presented at General Homma's trial included the fact that his headquarters was located only 500 yards from where the death march passed. He also admitted, according to testimony, that he had even driven down the road himself. Thus, it was reported, he had to have known what his men were doing on the blood-stained road.

Lieutenant General Homma's trial lasted five weeks during which time death march survivors told of the torturous treatment of prisoners. The defense counsel presented him as an officer dedicated to peace. Then before the verdict was announced, Homma, who spoke English, thanked the court for its courteous treatment during the trial. He was found guilty of the charges and hanged in April 1946 with very little criticism.

Also tried was the guard commander on the hell ship Oryoko

Maru that Father Duffy was aboard when it sunk. The commander was sentenced to death as was his interpreter. Four others were sent to prison. However, the commission acquitted the ship's captain, finding that he had no power to intervene.

Also targeted by the tribunal were members of the Kemptai, the secret police that acquitted Father Duffy, but was known for its brutality and arrogance, fatal beatings, beheadings and even poisonings of prisoners.

Just as terrible were the crimes of Japanese medical personnel who had murdered American prisoners, according to one enraged indictment, "by vivisecting them, mutilating and dissecting and removing parts from and otherwise desecrating bodies of said prisoners."

The first woman to be tried by the commission was an army nurse accused of participating in sadistic medical experiments.

Father Duffy (3rd from right) chats with Bishop Alter during a dinner that honored Toledo Diocese chaplains (at table) who returned from duty during World War II

(Photo courtesy of Diocese of Toledo, Ohio Archives)

Chapter XI
Assignment: New London

W hen Father Duffy was finally released from Walter Reed Hospital in Washington, D.C., in 1946, he made the trip back to Toledo to visit Bishop Alter. He made it clear that upon his return to the diocese, he wasn't interested in being assigned to a large parish, but would prefer a smaller one that's in need.

Bishop Alter selected the New London, Ohio parish and offered it to Father Duffy, who was residing at St. Ignatius at Momeneetown east of Toledo. The Bishop received this reply from him:

"My dear Bishop: This is to acknowledge your letter offering to appoint me to New London. I will be pleased to accept the appointment and await your pleasure. I may be contacted at Father Bishaps Momeneetown."

Father Duffy's appointment to the New London parish became official on 22 January 1947. He replaced Father Anthony Wortmann, who had been the pastor at New London for a year.

Father Duffy quickly got into the swing of things at Our Lady of Lourdes and launched an impressive renovation project. It included two new stained glass windows on both sides of the church, and a circular stained glass window at the rear of the altar with the inscription "For the Men of Bataan."

He also befriended two Hungarian displaced persons that were talented artists. They took two large pieces of Philippine mahogany and with one, carved an image of St. Joseph, who represents the labor force of the community. The other is a carving of Our Lady of Fatima, the Blessed Virgin Mary and Mother of God. She appeared to the three children, also on the carving, in Portugal six times from May 13 to October 13, 1917.

The two Hungarian artists, when their beautiful carvings were completed, decided to cast their lots in Chicago. Father Robert Haas, who was Our Lady of Lourdes pastor from 1995 to 2006, said that no one had ever heard from them afterward.

There is, strangely, a correlation between the Bataan Death March and the Blessed Virgin Mary's apparition at Fatima. As a sign that her message to the three children truly came from God, she performed a great miracle at Fatima on October 13, 1917. She had told the children she would perform a miracle on that date. Some 70,000 people watched that day when she made the sun rotate, grow large and then small, comet close to the people, and then retreat far away, and then the sun "danced". Every person there that day and was a witness testified that they saw the miracle. Even the non-believers went to their knees to seek forgiveness.

On the Bataan Death March, there were 50,000 Filipinos and 20,000 Americans, a total of 70,000 prisoners of the Japanese. There were many who were witnesses to the miracle of survival by Father Duffy.

In order to raise funds to build up Our Lady of Lourdes parish in New London, Father Duffy traveled around the country to give talks about his experiences, his brushes with death and the death march. He didn't, however, believe that it was necessary to go into all the gory details of the torture, sickness, and terrible conditions the POWs had to endure during more than three years of imprisonment, or to relive the brutality of the Japanese guards along that road to Camp O'Donnell.

In one of his talks, he said, " . . . If I thought Americans could be awakened by the recitation of the gory details and the beastiality of the Japanese soldiers and leaders during the Bataan Death March, I would tell of them, but I am not convinced it would help in establishing world peace. The world is better off not knowing the details . . ."

**Our Lady of Lourdes Catholic Church, New London, Ohio.
As seen in 2006.**

(Photo by Dan Murr)

Wood carvings created by friends of Father Duffy as part of the renovation of Our Lady of Lourdes Church. The carvings feature Our Lady of Fatima (top) and St. Joseph. (bottom)

(Photos by Dan Murr)

122

Others have been much more graphic about the inhumane conditions POWs were forced to contend with, the terrible conditions aboard the hell-ships and the trains. Prisoners were crammed into spaces so tight that it resulted in the suffocation deaths of hundreds to mention just one fatal problem.

In August 1948, Father Duffy attended the National Convention of the Disabled American Veterans in New York City and gave the principal address at the Memorial Service. He also introduced General Wainwright with the approval of his eminence Francis Cardinal Spellman, Archbishop of New York.

What Father Duffy heard General Wainwright say in his talk caught him completely by surprise. In a letter that he wrote shortly after the convention he said: "I had no idea that General J.M. Wainwright contemplated naming me his Chief of Staff. In fact, I was dumbfounded when he made the announcement after his acceptance speech. The tribute he paid me was something I never dreamed of, especially since he credited his decisions in Luzon and Bataan to my counsel. It was true that we spent a couple of hours together each night, except when I was covering some outfit that did not have a priest, and I knew he depended upon me, but I never expected that recognition."

The week before he attended the convention, Father Duffy was officially notified by the State Commander of the Forty and Eight, the honorary society of the Ohio American Legion, that he had been appointed the State Chaplain of the 40 & 8 for the 1951 fiscal year which commenced the next month (September).

Father Duffy never painted a bright future for the United States in his talks back then, but he usually would provide it with some hope.

One of his gloomy forecasts came in a speech before over a hundred members of the Rotary and Exchange clubs in Orrville, Ohio. Some who were in attendance believed that Father Duffy's bitterness was evident probably because he was a victim of the war.

He declared at the start of his talk that he believed this country was operating on the principle of a slot machine with everyone working to hit the jackpot. He said, "The greed and selfishness so evident today could indicate that we have learned nothing from our experience.

"I sometimes come to the tragic conclusion that the American people are not interested in the welfare of their country, but only in the welfare of themselves," he said. "And down this road lies disaster.

"We knew that war with the Japanese was coming from 1933 on, and yet we did nothing about it except to arm and implement the Japanese. Every truck that we saw on Bataan was either a Ford or a Chevrolet. All their guns bore the imprint 'U.S.A' and all their leather goods and much of their other equipment were stamped 'New England.' Most of their gasoline had been carried to them from our shores in our tankers.

"We had 16,000 troops in Hawaii before Pearl Harbor, and now we have 3,000. Congress authorized an armed force in the U.S. of 250,000 men as far back as 1920, but since August 1922, there had never been sufficient money appropriated up until the Japs struck to implement an army of more than 100,000. It looks to me as though we are doing the same thing again."

Then he struck another awesome fact when he said, "We didn't know anything was going to happen, eh?

"The Japanese began moving their troops to battle positions in early November 1941, but it was November 4 before a detachment of Marines arrived in the Philippines to reinforce the meagre forces we had there. And yet, we were surprised at Pearl Harbor!

"We were not in the Philippines to defend them, although we had pledged ourselves to safeguard them. We were in the Philippines to implement U.S. Policy in the Far East. You know now what that policy was worth."

Father Duffy also spoke of the complacency and conceit of the nation, "just as we are today," he said. "For years our Navy had boasted that they could destroy the Japanese Navy in six months. Well, the Japanese destroyed our Pacific fleet in less than one day and if they had been smart they could have landed on our West Coast and in cooperation with the 500,000 Japanese in this country, probably conquered the United States. Had they won the war, they wouldn't have owed any $250 million. They would have stripped this nation of its wealth, just as they did the Philippines, and would have shipped everything back to Japan and enslaved our people. I was a slave of the Japanese for three years. I can tell you what it means."

He used the United States Civil War as an example concerning America's boasts about its strength and greatness.

"The northern part of the country doesn't know what war means. It has never been invaded or its cities and countryside lay waste. South of the Mason and Dixon line, they can tell you something about it. They had an illustration in Sherman's march to the sea, with everything destroyed in the path of the Northern Army.

"If America doesn't realize that the only way to peace and understanding is to 'Love thy neighbor as thyself,' we are doomed as a nation. We are now undergoing confiscatory taxes and waste in government just as did ancient Rome, and Rome fell."

While others were highly critical of General MacArthur for leaving the "Battling Bastards of Bataan" far short of the six months supply of food and ammunition they were supposed to have had on hand, Father Duffy was highly complimentary of him.

The chaplain said that he had never known the man to make a wrong decision and declared that he was the greatest general of this age.

"He won the war without much help from Washington," Father Duffy said. "All he got was the spare parts."

Father Duffy went on to describe the Battle of the Philippines in which he paid unstinted praise to the heroism and valor of the handful of American troops that were engaged in that grim hour.

"We were ordered to make a delaying action for six months, but no one thought we would last six days," he said. "Yet in the great final battles of that campaign no less than 70,000 Japanese were killed. We lived for three months on seven ounces of food a day and when we finally gave up, there was scarcely a man who could stand on his feet.

"The tragedy of the world is that all the things we have developed have been and are being used for the destruction of man rather than for the benefit of man, and that's because, I think, that we do not recognize God. That's where we get into trouble.

"Our trouble is that we have had too many humans trying to be God. There was Franklin, and Uncle Joe, and Adolph and Benito,

125

not to mention Hirohito and Winnie. And, gentlemen, a man just can't be God. Unless we know this, and unless we live as God says we must live, there is no salvation for us on earth."

Father Duffy finished his address with an inspiring appeal for the nation to be prepared for any eventuality. He said that one of the main teachings of the founding fathers was that we must be strong in defense of our ideals, our rights and our possessions.

"You cannot know," he said "what it's like to be conquered until you have been conquered."

In his short time at New London*, Father Duffy became well-liked and well-known, not only as a Catholic priest, but also as a community leader. He helped in the drive to build the American Legion home in New London and was highly interested in the youth of the community. Each year, a scholarship is awarded to a student from New London High School from the Father Duffy Memorial Fund, and the most outstanding chaplain in the Legion is given the Father John E. Duffy Memorial plaque.

He was selected twice as Commander of the Broome-Wood American Legion Post 292 in New London (1947-48-49) and became so popular that he was elected chaplain of the American Legion at the National Convention in New York in 1952-53.

During 1953, Father Duffy became involved with the American Legion's 'Back to God' movement and continued his talks at different cities. He was summoned to Fort Wayne, Indiana by Carl J. Suedhoff, founder of the movement and a member of the American Legion. When he finished his talk, an editorial was written in the Fort Wayne News-Sentinel on 18 May. This is what was written:

Father Duffy's Magnificent 'Sermon'

It is perfectly obvious that there is something terribly wrong with the world today, and many have undertaken to tell us just what it is, and just what to do to right it. Regrettably however, few have been able to acquire the discerning insight, born of long first-hand contact with manifestations of the motivating forces of the world

* Information provided by Paul Krupp's Welcome to Potluck newsletter, March, 1986.

today, to qualify for such an exacting messianic role.

On this general background of inadequacy of assaying of cause and subscribing of remedy, we have just heard the most convincing appraisal of both the cause of, and the cure for, what's wrong with the world today, that we have ever heard. It came from the inspired lips, warm humane-minded heart, and courageous God-fearing soul of the National Chaplain of the American Legion – the Rev. Father John E. Duffy, one of America's great war heroes, brought here by American Legion Post 47 in behalf of the Legion's 'Back to God' Movement, which, incidentally, was founded by a Fort Wayne legionaire, Carl J. Suedhoff.

From the vantage point of years of first-hand study of the nations of the world – notably nearly a decade in the Far East, action-packed service in World War II in which he was wounded six times, and from the soul-searing, body-wracking experiences of death marches and years of mental and physical torture at the hands of unspeakably cruel and cunning captors, Father Duffy told Fort Wayne what is wrong with the world today. Simply, he said, it is an uncanny, misanthropic worldwide philosophy of brazen godlessness, exploitation of others, and withal having everyone reduced to the lowest common denominator of feeding at the public trough. The cause of what is wrong with the world, as so realistically evaluated by Father Duffy, just as simply reflects its own only possible cure.

Dramatically outlining the mighty contending ideological forces in the world today, the inspired clerical head of the American Legion said:

"There are two great systems of thought struggling for survival in the world today.

"One is the philosophy of a universal collectivism, comprising a material universe, divorced from God.

"The other is an individual nationalism, recognizing the dignity of man as a creative child of God with certain inherent rights springing from his nature as a human being. This system places its hope in a belief in God and our fellow man."

The famous priest-soldier verified his appraisal of the cause of the world's sad state with a recital of how the same Godless philosophy of collectivism that obtains today, inevitably destroyed numerous other civilizations in the past, beginning with the Judaic or Israelite civilization of Biblical times, and continuing through the Babylonian and Roman empires, the reign of Charlemagne to the Sixteenth Century with the 30 years war in Germany. With dramatic documentation, Father Duffy provided how the decline and final extermination of all these civilizations was due to the departure from God and the espousal of a materialistic philosophy predicated on exploitation that paradoxically employed the technique of having everybody eat (no matter how badly) "at the public trough." Always there arose, he said, (just as in Russia today) one nation that took upon itself to administer the Godless philosophy of materialistic exploitation and common reliance for a bare, frugal existence, upon the all-powerful state.

All these once great civilizations, the National Legion Chaplain said, died of the same common obvious cause, but still the world did not learn, citing that since the Sixteenth Century, European nations have been exploiting East Asia and that "in the past 500 years, most Europeans have considered it their inherent right to live off the Oriental. He emphasized the great difference between the American and European treatment of the East Asian in the past half century, and pointed out that the Oriental can be made capable of the most diabolic cruelty, but that he can also be capable of the most profound kindness, cooperation and helpfulness toward those he has had reason to learn to like and respect. He cited how our firm but non-exploitative and humane policy in the Philippines had earned for us the lasting friendship of the Asiatics there, which was reflected in World War II, when the natives, at great risk of their own lives, nursed death march victims like himself, back to life and did everything possible that they could for the United States.

Father Duffy cited our tragic error in losing this respect and kindly feeling of the Oriental through the degrading spectacle of weakness of our ghastly misadventure in Korea and our continual desperate efforts toward trying to save the British Empire and other European imperial nations for further exploitation of the Asiatics.

"Despite their contempt for us, as we again expressed the other day by Mr. Atlee when he said our Constitution was no good, we have virtually insisted that the British take our billions to try to save their empire and another dying civilization that it represents, so as to enable them to continue to exploit the Asiatic. Moreover, we fought the Revolutionary War to shake off the British yoke only now to become their most loyal and obeisant subject."

The noted Chaplain declared that we have been too pre-occupied trying to save moribund European nations, dead empires and another dying civilization, realistically to apply our highly successful policy in the Philippines to the rest of Asia, which he said would be just as susceptible to it, if we but inspired its regard and respect, as General MacArthur did, and would have continued to have, had he been given the opportunity. He said that the hope of America and the world still depends on our concentration of our traditional American philosophy upon East Asia and keeping its greatest fund of "undeveloped natural resources in the world," from getting into the hands of the Russians.

Repeatedly, Father Duffy referred for support of his convictions, to remarks of the Rev. E.W. Weber, Lutheran minister and chaplain at the Veterans Hospital, who introduced him, and who also served for years as an Army chaplain. The program was a magnificent inter-faith reconsecration to the principles of the Fatherhood of God, the Fellowship of Man and sterling God-fearing Americanism. And Father Duffy's "sermon" was one of the finest we have ever heard."

Top: Stained glass window at the rear of Our Lady of Lourdes CatholicChurch at New London, Ohio installed by Father Duffy and inscribed "For the Men of Bataan".
(Photo by Dan Murr)

Bottom: Father Duffy (back row, center) is shown with the 1948 Communion at Our Lady of Lourdes Parish.
(Photo courtesy of Our Lady of Lourdes Parish, New London, Ohio)

Chapter XII
The End Time

Father Duffy had definitely distinguished himself during his eleven years as pastor at Our Lady of Lourdes. He had completely renovated the church, and installed that special stained glass window at the rear and top of the altar inscribed "For the Men of Bataan." As a matter of fact, he dedicated the entire project to those men. All of them, not just the survivors.

In Father Duffy's time at the parish, he had more than sixty men, women and young people converted to the Catholic faith. A sizable number when the size of the village of New London, a population of only a little over 1,600, is considered.

One of Father Duffy's most dramatic conversions took place at New London Hospital where Pete Clemmons, a local postal worker who had served in the Army's 145th Infantry during World War I, called him. He had been an infantryman at first, then transferred to a machine gun unit and became a machine gunner. The 145th was part of the 37th Ohio Division, a National Guard unit under the command of Major General Charles S. Farnsworth and engaged with the French in Flanders and at the Escaut River just prior to the end of hostilities on 11 November 1918.

Pete had been born on 22 June 1887 and raised in Fitchville, a small farming hamlet located five miles west of New London. Before he enlisted in the Army, he helped his dad with the farm. He entered the service on 28 May 1917 and trained at Camp Sheridan in Montgomery, Alabama.

Pete's outfit also had been involved in the Meuse-Argonne offensive that began on 26 September. At one point, the Germans had surrounded his machine gun nest and trapped him there for about seventy-two hours. His position was rescued when American troops overran the area.

Pete remained in the Army until his discharge on 22 April 1919 and then returned home. He married and he and his wife Anna had five girls and a son. They eventually moved to New London where they raised their children.

Father Duffy and Pete became close friends through meetings at the Broome-Wood American Legion post in New London. Pete was not Catholic at that time, but he had brought a Rosary home from the war that he had taken from a dead French soldier.

"I remember having that rosary around the house," said Ardis Budd, one of Pete's daughters. "I think us kids probably played with it."

Pete suffered his first major heart attack in 1948 and hospitalized at the Veterans Hospital in Brecksville. He had a more serious attack again in 1954, and after he had been in the hospital several weeks, he began to ask for John. Anna, his wife, didn't think much of it because she knew he and John were good friends.

He finally spoke to Alma White, the nurse on duty, and told her that he'd like to see John. She immediately called Father Duffy to come to the hospital right away. Father Duffy began to talk with Pete and visited him there for a few days. Then he baptized Pete.

Afterward Father Duffy told him, "Now Pete, you'll go to Heaven, and I've been a priest most of my life and I don't know where I'm going!"

After Father Duffy had tended to the conversion, Pete always called him Father John.

During Father Duffy's visits to the old red brick hospital, Ardis finally asked him one day, "Why a priest?"

In his subtle sense of humor, he answered, "I'm ugly." He paused for a few moments and gave her a brief answer. "I had a girlfriend, but it didn't work out, so I became a priest."

Ardis and her mother stayed at the hospital with Pete. He

hadn't been placed on any medication, only oxygen. Then one day after Pete's baptism, he looked at Anna and Ardis and asked,

"Where'd he go?"

"Who," Anna asked.

"The man who came through the window," Pete answered.

"What did he want?" she asked.

"A drink of water."

"What did he look like?"

"Oh like any other man . . . dressed in a white robe."

Pete had been in the hospital for twenty-seven days and on 20 April, he passed away.

Janette, another of Pete's daughters, remembered that her dad was not what people call a religious man. "But in his heart he was," she said.

Father Duffy had given Pete the last rites of the church, and after his funeral, he told Janette and the family, "Pray to your dad, not for him."

Later on, Janette again spoke with Father Duffy. He told her, "Even though I was in that hellish death march, I knew the Lord had some plan for me and that I was sent to New London to save your dad's soul."

"He said it with a straight face and smiled at me like God just directed him to say that," she said. "In those days we didn't kiss a priest, but I sure wanted to."

After Pete's death, his wife Anna, Ardis and her husband, and another daughter, Joyce, all took instructions to convert to Catholicism. That was the Marian year and Father Duffy often spoke of Pete Clemmons at Mass and about the "Miracle that happened in our little town."

But now, four years later, something had begun to happen to Father Duffy's physical well being. It seemed that all the wounds – the death march, the bayoneting, the hell-ship disasters, the beatings and torture and sickness he suffered through during his prisoner-of-war years were coming back to haunt him once again. In a letter to The Bishop of Toledo, Most Reverend George J. Rehring on 6 January 1956, Father Duffy made a special request:

"I would like to have your permission to be away from my parish from six weeks to two months for the purpose of making a pilgrimage to the Shrine of Our Lady of Guadalupe in Mexico, and for recuperating in the Southwest.

"I was retired from the Army over nine years ago for enemy inflicted disability – I had been wounded six times in action, and found 80 percent disabled. My physical condition has not improved, and there is never a time that I am not in pain. This condition has become more acute, and these northern winters are difficult for me. I would like to be away from six weeks to two months, depending upon the relief that's secured in a warmer climate. I am not complaining about my pains. I never speak of them to anyone. I know no one is interested, and that unless one can see a leg off, or an arm missing, they cannot comprehend. I'm not looking for sympathy. I state these facts merely so that you will understand the request.

"The only years I instruct a considerable number of converts are the years I make a pilgrimage to Guadalupe. And I have concluded that the time taken to visit Our Lady's shrine has always made those years more profitable.

"I cannot plan on leaving before the 18th or 20th of this month as I must attend a National Committee meeting of the American Legion in Indianapolis next week."

Three days later, the Very Reverend Robert J. Yates, secretary to Bishop Rehring, responded with approval of Father Duffy's request and noted, "His Excellency deeply sympathizes with you in the physical disabilities that you suffer as a result of your service on behalf of our country. He knows that ailments such as yours may be almost intolerable even though they do not appear to an observer. He hopes you will find relief in a temporary visit in a warmer climate."

All arrangements were made and Father Duffy was able to make the Legion National Committee meeting. Then he departed on the Guadalupe pilgrimage.

She called herself the Mother of the True God and appeared to a poor Indian named Juan Diego at Tepeyac, a hill located northwest

134

of Mexico City, in 1531. She told him to tell the Bishop to build a temple on the site and left an imprint of herself on Juan's Tilma, a cape made of poor cactus cloth. It should have deteriorated twenty years later, but 474 years afterward, it shows no sign of decay and defies all scientific explanation of its origin. That image was enough to convince the Bishop.

They say that her eyes reflect the image that was in front of her in 1531.

Father Duffy had taken a number of pilgrims and converts from his parish in New London to the apparition site of Our Lady of Guadalupe. There has been a list of incredible miracles, cures and interventions attributed to her, and each year, some 10 million visit her Basilica. That makes her Mexico City home the most popular Marian Shrine in the world and the most visited Catholic Church in the world next to The Vatican.

Only those who were very close to Father Duffy were aware of his problems, but finally, on 18 October 1957, Father Duffy sent this letter to Bishop Rehring:

"About three weeks ago, I had a tumor removed from my back. On analysis it was found to have a low-grade malignancy. The doctor advised that I go back to the hospital and have the tissue out all around it so as to prevent a recurrence. This I did last Tuesday. I came home from the hospital this noon.

"They removed about two inches of skin and tissue from all sides of the area where the tumor had been and cleared the flesh out to the muscles. They think they have everything out. It, of course, necessitated the removal of quite a hunk of meat, so maybe they have eliminated the beefs. Outside of being a little uncomfortable, I'm getting along alright."

Bishop Rehring was encouraged by Father Duffy's report and in his response said, "May the Divine High Priest who is also the Divine Physician grant you a complete and speedy recovery."

But the news to the bishop from Father Duffy on 25 October was not good.

"They removed nine stitches the other day and the laboratory report came back," he wrote. "In analyzing the hunk of meat they took from my back, they found malignant cells under the tumor that was removed a month ago and also under a growth that had been removed in November 1956. The report on the November '56 operation had at that time been negative. They hope that they have eliminated the cause, but, of course, cannot be certain. The wound is using syrum and is dressed every other day. Though it's uncomfortable, we are able to carry on.

"It will take time for it to heal, and to indicate whether there will be a recurrence."

During the next three months, Father Duffy didn't improve. By the time Christmas arrived, he had developed what he thought was a severe case of neuritis in the right side of his back opposite from where the surgery was performed the previous October.

He began to take treatment from one of his doctors, but just before New Year's Eve, he wrote to Bishop Rehring again and said, "The pain became so terrific that I was unable to be comfortable in any position. I tried to get help for the New Year's Masses and succeeded in getting Father Gasper to come and say the second one. I managed to struggle through the first, but with great difficulty. I had the Missionaries say the two Masses last Sunday as I was unable.

"The doctor is giving me four different pills four times a day and two different shots every other day," he wrote. "The pain has eased some but the trouble is not yet eliminated. I guess the nerves have to be healed and that's a slow process. He doesn't know how long it will take. The cause probably is the war injuries to the back and unknown anxieties. It's much better though than it was.

"When the doctor gets this nerve damage cleared up, but not before January 20th, I would like permission to go to the Southwest for from six weeks to two months to see if a warmer and a dryer climate will help with rest and relaxation.

"I've made arrangements for Father Paul Hill, MSC to cover the place for me in the event you grant me this permission, and I would also like to have a celebrant."

Three weeks later, Father Duffy told the Bishop that the neuritis had become so bad that "I have not been able to take off for the Southwest. When . . . and if . . .I should recover sufficiently to make a trip to a warmer and dryer climate, I will let you know.

"Dr. Marley is sending me to Crile (VA Hospital, Cleveland) for a complete checkup, and treatment of the neuritis," he told Bishop Rehring. "The pathological slides on the fall operation and all other data are going with me. The checkup will take at least a week."

A month later, in February 1958, Father Duffy sent a request to Bishop Rehring to go to California. The response from the Bishop was positive and Father Duffy, who continued his physical decline, sent this letter.

"I am grateful, that if I get out of here, it will be alright for me to go to California. That's what the doctors (at Crile Hospital) recommend.

"I find that I do not have neuritis, but cancer on two of the vertebraes of the back which is causing the excruciating pain that drugs alleviate only for a short time. In addition," he said "the skin cancer removed last fall has spread very rapidly and there are many tumors around the trunk of my body. There is no cure, but they are now trying by x-ray to kill the tumors on the spine to alleviate the pain, and they're of the opinion that all of them came from this source. They took a tumor from my breast, which was the same type as removed by Dr. Marley last fall. They have made many slides of it, which have been sent to all the research centers in the country for their opinion and experience in treatment. It's rare, a type about which they do not know too much, except that it's called wild and speedy in its activity."

Father Duffy explained that they would try to stop the pain and slow down the progress, "but it cannot be cured," he said. "It may be weeks, months . . . but hardly more than a year. It'll be at least three weeks before it's known what can be done here."

Then he wrote, "I have had a session with my confessor, and have been anointed, so that nature might have favorable environment to operate.

"When I know the complete picture, I will send you my resignation from New London and I hope you keep the parish for a diocesan priest.

"As soon as any loose ends are taken care of at New London, I will fly to Carmel, California and spend my last days there.

"I would appreciate very much if you could see your way to give some consideration to John Bardis of New London who is finishing Philosophy this year at Mt. St. Mary's. He has a special talent for languages and I consider him very sincere and dependable with a very high sense of responsibility.

"If I die before I go to California, bury me in New London, and if I get to California, I will buy a lot in the Monterey Cemetery. I prefer to be buried where-ever I die. I do not wish to be shipped around the country. I'd also appreciate it if you would write to the Bishop of Monterey-Fresno if I am able to go to California. Let him know I am in his diocese.

"Begging your pardon for any offenses I have committed against you, assuring you of my efforts to offer these pains in reparation for all my transgressions, I ask your blessing and that God's will be done."

An incident happened during the next two weeks, only no one but Father Duffy and another person knew about it. A benefactor came forth to Father Duffy to pave the way for him to make a special pilgrimage to Lourdes, France. The benefactor to this day remains anonymous, and apparently encouraged Father to take this journey.

Lourdes, of course, is where apparitions of the Blessed Virgin Mary occurred starting on 11 February 1858. Bernadette Soubirous, a young, poor, sickly peasant girl 14 years of age, had gone to collect firewood when she heard the sound of the wind, then saw a light that became the silhouette of a girl as young as herself. The girl smiled at Bernadette and invited her to pray.

A week later, the young girl asked Bernadette if she would be willing to come here for two weeks.

"Yes," Bernadette answered.

"I don't promise to make you happy in this world, but in the other."

At one of the apparitions, Bernadette was invited to scrape in the mud at the back of the Grotto until a spring came forth. Like pigs and other animals, she crawled there on her hands and knees, mimed the condition of sinners, and then she drank and washed herself in the water.

The water of Lourdes is ordinary water, a sign that Mary uses to remind people of the words of Jesus. "If anyone thirsts, let him come to me. Let the one come and drink who believes in me."

The word is that if you are in Lourdes, it is not by accident.

Millions of pilgrims and visitors come to Lourdes from all around the world. Some are believers, some are merely curious, but many come to be healed, physically and spiritually, and miracles happen there every day. Some are miraculously healed, but many more are not cured of their affliction. They receive the great and precious grace of lovingly embracing and carrying the cross Our Lord has given them.

Thus Father Duffy received an opportunity to make the trip to Lourdes and wrote this letter to the Bishop, who had apparently asked him the name of the benefactor.

"It is the desire of my benefactor that he remain anonymous.

"I said mass this morning only with great difficulty. I will not be able to make any public appearance in the church tomorrow, but will try to say a private mass early.

"I will attempt to do nothing here until the effects of the treatment have been determined which will be in two or three weeks.

"I hope to get away from here tomorrow and will notify you upon my return (from Lourdes).

"I would greatly appreciate that there be no publicity whatsoever about my situation and planned trip."

Plans also were under way for Father Duffy's move to California. A message from Monsignor Weger revealed that it included taking his niece, Dorothy Vogel, who has been his housekeeper since about 1938, with him.

Dorothy's sister said that there was no relationship between her family and Father Duffy, but that her family had been good friends of the father for years.

The monsignor also said that Father Duffy's parents, Mr. And Mrs. James E. Duffy, were living in Lafayette, Indiana, but were elderly and ill and had not been told of their son's condition.

After Father Duffy returned from Lourdes, he wrote this letter on 10 March 1958 to Bishop Rehring. It spoke of his illness and briefly about his pilgrimage to Lourdes.

"We arrived back at the Cleveland Airport on Wednesday afternoon, 5 March, and the next day reported in at Crile Veterans Hospital where we were checked and put on a temporary pass late Saturday afternoon, 8 March.

"They informed me that they were studying the results of some new drugs that had been successful, with reference to my rare active skin cancer tumors, and that they would telephone me the results on Monday.

"The doctors called this evening and told me they thought this new drug, which they want to try and would administer over three days with a six-day observation period, should be taken. They desire that I rest here this week and report into Crile Veterans Hospital Monday morning, 17 March. I will be there until 25 March after which they will release me to Letterman (General Hospital, San Francisco).

"I have agreed to take the treatment and will report there on Monday morning, 17 March.

"I have said private masses here, but have not been able to make any public appearance.

"The trip to Lourdes and back was painful and difficult, but I am delighted that I was able to make it. I said Mass at the Cript the morning I arrived, and Friday at the Cript and Saturday at the Grotto. I performed all the prescribed works for the pilgrimage, including taking the bath in the water. The water of Lourdes, as the attendants submerge you, does something for one that cannot be described.

"We were fourteen hours late getting to Paris, but Father McGoohan met us and took us to the hotel. We had diplomatic immunity for some reason or other.

"Back in Paris on Sunday morning, Father McGoohan showed us some of Paris. General Hodes, the Supreme American Commander, called us from Heidelburg, and on Monday evening, personal friends of Cardinal Tisserant had us to dinner and told us of Cardinal Stritch's new appointment in the Vatican Curia.

"I got a definite pickup from Lourdes," Father Duffy wrote. "The peace of soul was well worth all the physical difficulties of the trip and we were able to manage without any strong drugs, not taking an APC more often than once in three hours.

"I will be here this week, but will attempt no public appearance," he said.

"I am now in a steel harness that must be worn whenever I walk or ride, and the ride from here to Crile is all I can take in a car. In a plane, I must wear it going up and coming down, and then I can take it off.

"I will plan on leaving here around 27 March and will send in the formal resignation letter.

"Father Robert Knoefle will take the Class reunion that I was to have and has probably contacted you and told you and asked you to come to Landeck rather than New London. Father Werner is going to help him.

"Saturday I received a very nice letter from General MacArthur. He expressed his concern over my health and his appreciation of my service in the last war. I do not know who told him I was sick."

Only five days had passed when Father Duffy officially severed his connection to Our Lady of Lourdes parish at New London, Ohio and with the Diocese of Toledo and Bishop Rehring.

This is his official letter of resignation.

"My dear Bishop Rehring:

I herewith submit my resignation as Pastor of Our Lady of Lourdes Parish, New London, Ohio, effective March 27th, because of total physical disability which will make it impossible for me to look after the care of souls here.

"I request to be put on the retired list and to be given an indefinite leave of absence. I plan to reside at Carmel Valley, California, as the medics advise that I live in a tropical climate. May I request that you notify Bishop Aloysius J. Willinger, C.S.S.R., of Monterey-Fresno.

"I give the following articles to Our Lady of Lourdes Parish and they are to remain there as long as they can serve any useful purpose. One Philco TV with rotary antenna; one General Electric deep freeze; one set of Catholic encyclopedias; one hundred books to serve as a nucleus for a parish library; one hand hammered chalice with stem of wheat sheaves and grape vines and grapes; one sixteen pound, solid silver, hand-hammered Monstrance adorned with thirteen amethysts, with the inner luna made of purest gold.

"The Monstrance was made for me seven years ago in Mexico City by Senor Margo. Six workmen worked a month on it. Their bench was a crate and their table a tree stump. Mr. and Mrs. H.M. Schonecker of this parish were with me on this trip and will verify anything concerning it. The Monstrance cost me about one thousand American dollars. It is a combination of three old Spanish Monstrances. Several jewelers have appraised it and put its value between $15,000.00 and $17,000.00, and then affirmed they could not replace it for that. The crown on the plaque of Our Lady of Fatima is also of solid silver and made by Senor Margo. The seven pearls in it were brought from the Sulu Seas during my tours in the Philippine Islands. It was presented to Our Lady on the occasion of the twenty-fifth anniversary of my ordination.

"Asking your blessing, and a prayerful remembrance, I beg the privilege of remaining, Respectfully yours in Christ, /S/ Rev. John E. Duffy."

Obviously Bishop Rehring had no alternative but to accept "with regret and a certain amount of reluctance" Father Duffy's resignation from Our Lady of Lourdes Parish.

Bishop Rehring offered in his letter of 17 March to Father Duffy:

"Accepting a resignation always occasions a feeling of sadness. We realize that the moment will come for us when we can no longer perform our duties as priests. However, we all hope that God will grant us the privilege of serving Him until an old age. That hope, of course, should be accompanied by a complete resignation to God's Will. You have already expressed such a sentiment and thought, and now similarly actuated, and not merely because I have no other choice, I accede to your expressed desire."

He continued, "Let me offer you my heartfelt appreciation for the splendid services you have rendered to the parish more or less habitually with great cost to you physically. Your self-sacrifices and generosity also have put the parish in its present flourishing condition. Your goal for the spiritual well-being of all the people in the territory of the parish has been a source of real edification and consolation."

Bishop Rehring went on to honor Father Duffy's gifts to the parish and called the Monstrance and Chalice "both artistic masterpieces of the precious metalsmith's craftsmanship" and said that this "places us in even larger debt to you."

Father Duffy acknowledged Bishop Rehring's letter on 26 March after he returned from Crile Veterans Hospital. He had been checked for results of the new drug doctors had started to use. Father Duffy would be en route to California shortly and be attached to Letterman General Hospital at The Presidio in San Francisco. There, he would be checked every seven days for three weeks on the new drug. The full effects would not be known until that time. After that, he would report each month or more often if any change in his condition was noted.

The only effects of the treatments to date, according to Father Duffy, were that there were no new tumors and no enlargement of present ones. The x-ray on the vertebrae indicated no change.

"It's the pressure of these tumors on a main nerve that causes the pain and suffering," said Father Duffy. "The doctors did not hope for this much a month ago."

Father Duffy expressed his regrets that his health "forces me to leave the diocese."

The night before Father Duffy left for California, about 250 parishioners and friends attended a reception to say goodbye to the ailing priest in the basement of Our Lady of Lourdes Church in New London.

A friend asked him about his future plans.

"I just want to get well," Father Duffy said. "I'll just take it easy in the sunshine."

It was April, and Father Duffy was now at Carmel Valley, California. He was ready to move into his new residence that Dorothy Vogel, his niece and long-time housekeeper, had been preparing for him. She had been with Father Duffy since before the war and had gone with him to the Philippine Islands.

Despite Father Duffy's illness, he managed to tease Dorothy after he arrived in Carmel Valley about "you've finally got your pink living room." That wasn't exactly what Father Duffy had in mind for that room. It actually was a salmon color, but when the sun set across the Pacific Ocean, it looked pink.

Father Duffy's downhill trek became steeper and faster and on 24 April 1958, he sent a shaky hand-written note to Bishop Rehring back at the Diocese of Toledo.

"Just a note to let you know I am in Letterman General Hospital. I became paralyzed from the waist down on April 13th. Called Fort Ord and they shipped me here by military ambulance.

"I was just ready to move into a Carmel Valley home when this happened.

"I am receiving the best of care, but it's not known whether I will ever walk again. They do not yet know if the interior of the (spinal) cord is damaged beyond self-repair.

"My sufferings and difficulties are offered for your intentions.

"Pray for me."

It was the last time the bishop would hear from Father Duffy. The next communication to Bishop Rehring came in the form of a Western Union telegram sent at 11:59 p.m. on 4 June 1958:

"Father John E. Duffy of your diocese, retired Army chaplain, died at 0930 hours 4 June 1958 at Letterman Army Hospital, San Francisco, California. Solemn High Requiem Mass will be at 1000 hours Friday 6 June 1958 at Chapel of Our Lady, Presidio of San Francisco and interment at San Francisco National Cemetery, Presidio of San Francisco, California.

"Chaplain (Lieutenant Colonel) S.J. Baumgart, Catholic Chaplain, was with him at time of death."

On a slope overlooking San Francisco Bay, a small plot of sacred ground inside The Presidio National Cemetery holds the body of Colonel John Edward Duffy, retired due to health issues, and a highly decorated U.S. Army Chaplain. He has been at rest in this special place since 6 June 1958.

His niece, the late Dorothy Vogel Baltes who also had been his housekeeper during his 11 years as pastor at Our Lady of Lourdes parish in New London, said it had been reserved for someone very distinguished. At the time of his death that day in 1958 at Letterman General Hospital at The Presidio, she said that this place, surrounded by Monterrey Cypress trees on rolling California terrain, had been so designated for him.

To the northeast out in San Francisco Bay lies Angel Island, an immigration station; the Marin Headlands jut out into the bay, and to the left you can see the high towers of the Golden Gate Bridge. Off to the right loom the infamous Alcatraz Island, once a military strong hold, military prison and later a federal penitentiary that housed such public enemies as Al Capone and Machine Gun Kelly. Perhaps it's a grim reminder of Father Duffy's days as a Japanese prisoner of war, of the terror and torture and pain he suffered through, how he persevered, then eventually arrived at his final place of peaceful rest.

One lone medal provides testimony to most of that pain, the Purple Heart with five oak leaf clusters that denotes the six times he was wounded. He was recommended for the Navy Cross, the Silver Star and Distinguished Service Cross but did not receive them. It does not tell the whole brutal story of his capture near Mariveles, or the two times he was bayoneted by Japanese guards on the Bataan Death March, then left for dead on the second occasion. And it does not tell about the torture he endured, or the aid and comfort he provided his fellow American and Filipino POWs, or of his betrayal by a fellow soldier, an angry Filipino, to the Japanese; or the terror of the three hell-ships he was aboard with other American POWs, of their strafing and bombing by American planes and of their deaths.

It did include his prayers, reconciliation and last rites for those who died . . . some of those in Father Duffy's comforting arms.

Father Duffy's astounding journey had finally come to an end.

**Display case inside the Broome-Wood American Legion Post 292
at New London, Ohio where Father Duffy's medals and other
memorabilia can be seen.**
(Photo by Dan Murr)

Chapter XIII

Father Duffy's Month's Mind Mass

On the last day of June 1958, the passing of Father John Edward Duffy was not quite a month old. But on the morning of 30 June, Bishop George J. Rehring marked the time with the Month's Mind Mass at Our Lady of Consolation Church at Carey, Ohio.

The Month's Mind Mass is a special, lovely Catholic devotional, the celebration of a Mass four weeks after the death of a loved one. Its history dates back to medieval times and later in England. Special care is taken so on the 30th day after death, Mass is offered for the repose of the soul of the deceased.

This is how Bishop Rehring marked Father Duffy's month-old death with the Month's Mind Mass:

"Never was there a time in the extraordinary career of Father Duffy when he reached a greater height than in the weeks immediately preceding his death. All of his patriotic activities and his heroic services for God and country were eclipsed and thrown into the shadows by his exemplary confrontation of certain death within the proximate future.

"No deed of valor performed by him (and many had been performed by him) equaled the magnitude of his courage in the face of an incurable disease. His acknowledgment of his complete dependence upon his Lord God Creator, his unreserved submission to God's Will, his sincere acceptance of his disappointments and sufferings, must have been an occasion of edification and of sincere admiration for all who came into contact with him in those final weeks.

`The story of Father Duffy's years in Military Service is so well-known to you that it need not be recalled here this morning. Indeed, his sufferings and afflictions during and after World War II have been told so graphically and frequently that they are indelibly inscribed upon our memories. The pain from the wounds inflicted upon him at Bataan, which were never entirely healed, was as much as he was able to bear. However, he bore his cross without complaint and with admirable patience. Although his disability was of high percentage, he forced himself to discharge parish responsibilities and to lecture frequently before military and civic gatherings.

"Shortly after the first of the current year he informed me of his deteriorating condition and of the advancing seriousness of his terminal malady. At Crile Hospital where I visited him in February he mentioned that he was being pressed by an intimate friend to undertake a pilgrimage to Lourdes in this, the Centenary year of the Apparitions of St. Bernadette. This pilgrimage he actually made with our consent, approval and blessing. At his request there was to be no publicity given to this pious journey, at least during his lifetime. However, as we surmised from the beginning, it was not to escape publicity altogether. Knowledge of it soon spread amongst his friends and acquaintances. Personally I made a first public reference to it after the press announcement of his death in the military hospital at San Francisco. The one fact that I am pleased to have an opportunity to bring out this morning is his exemplary resignation to the Divine Will especially in the closing days of his remarkable career.

"Speaking of his approaching pilgrimage to Lourdes, he said that undoubtedly his friends were hoping for a miracle. However, he wished me to understand that he was going to Lourdes mainly to obtain the Grace of remaining resigned to God's Will and to beg for the Grace of final perseverance. He stood ready, without any reservation, to serve his Creator, to glorify his Creator, to spend himself in the service of his Creator in the manner and for the length of time decreed by his Creator; he was also ready to answer the final summons and to yield his soul to his Creator. It was in this spirit of beautiful resignation that he returned from Our Lady's Shrine at Lourdes where he had the profound consolation and joy of offering the Holy Sacrifice of the Mass on three successive days.

"I am sure that every one of you understands clearly why this last period of his life brings out the greatness of the soul of this, our departed brother priest. He left us with many memories – the most precious of which was his docile acceptance of God's Will in death. May that memory never be effaced and may it fortify us in trials and tribulations. May it inspire us to work untiringly for the grace to have and to maintain an unwavering resignation to the Divine Will in every situation and especially at the supreme moment of death. May the Lord God, our Creator, our Heavenly Father, our Divine Saviour, the Holy Spirit of Love grant him eternal rest, the peace and the happiness of the blessed."

On 5 November 1998, forty years after the passing of Father Duffy, he, along with 26 other veterans that composed the class of 1998, was selected for induction into the Ohio Veterans Hall of Fame in Columbus, Ohio.

The Month's Mind Mass for Father Duffy was taken from his files at the Diocese of Toledo Archives on 6 June 2006.

Epilogue

First word: How?

How could any man stand all the pain and suffering, wounds and torture, the sickness and constant look at the face of death that Father John Duffy went through those three and a half years and still live?

Maybe Father Duffy wasn't just any man.

How could Jesus stand the scourging, the pain and suffering that He was forced to endure? He was sent here by the Almighty Father, human in nature, divine and with a distinct purpose.

Father Duffy did not face the same purpose, but it could have been to set an example of perseverance, dedication and love for his fellow man.

The Congressional Medal of Honor recommendation for him . . . why was it rejected? Perhaps because there were other chaplains who experienced similar pain and suffering, but died in the process and not so recognized due to the fact that their service and performance of their duties beyond expectations were unknown in many instances.

Father Duffy and the other men of the cloth were not hunting medals or glory. They were trying to save souls, ease their pain, and send them joyfully on their way to Heaven.

If there is a purpose for this book, it's not clear at this moment. It seems, however, that perhaps, even in the rejection of the recommendation for the Congressional Medal of Honor, those who rejected it had no clear reason, either. It could be to give the young and old a glimpse of a true hero at a time in our country's history when love of country and love of our fellow man is somehow not appreciated.

In comparing Father Duffy's three and a half years of pain and suffering to that of Jesus Christ, it points to a single word and one of the prayers on the Chaplet of St. Michael: Perseverance.

The eighth Celestial Choir of Angels prayer is: By the intercession of St. Michael and the Celestial Choir of Archangels, may the Lord give us PERSEVERANCE in faith and all good works in order to gain the glory of Paradise.

Throughout Father Duffy's pain and suffering of surrender, the death march on Bataan, the bayoneting, the Kemptai court-martial, torture by his captors, the hell-ships and sickness, and the constant staring into the face of death, he miraculously persevered and never lost his faith and trust in God.

His pain and suffering continued on after World War II and ended in the form of cancer, until it finally paralyzed him and did what his Japanese captors must have wanted to do – it killed him.

His legacy might be to set an example for the world, to persevere in faith and to love one another. Father Duffy did it, and he did it gloriously. His reward must be great in Heaven.

Near the end, he wrote to Bishop Rehring and expressed his regrets that his health forced him to leave the diocese. "I have tried to give of myself and my substance while here," he wrote. "I have not talked about my work for I have always thought that it could speak for itself. I have never been one to give explanations of my actions for I have always been convinced a friend did not need an explanation and an enemy would not believe me. I forgive all those who have injured me, and ask forgiveness of all those whom I may have injured, and ask God to have mercy on me."

The Author

In the Aftermath...

We are the battling bastards of Bataan,
No mama, no papa, no Uncle Sam;
No aunts, no uncles, no cousins, no nieces;
No pills, no planes, no artillery pieces;
And nobody gives a damn.

~ *Frank Hewlett,*
Associated Press International

Bataan Peninsula

This peninsula sticks out in Manila Bay overlooking Corregidor Island. After the "Fall Of Bataan," a series of infamous Death Marches began in Mariveles and ended in Capas, Tarlac. Many American and Filipino soldiers died along the way. The entire historic march can be traced by following markers. At San Fernando, American soldiers were crammed into boxcars and transported to the infamous Camp O'Donnell. On April 7, 2000, former death march survivors and representatives of the Philippine government dedicated the "Battling Bastards Of Bataan" memorial at the Camp O'Donnell site. Paid for by members of the Battling Bastards Of Bataan organization, it honors the over 1,600 Americans who perished there from inhumane treatment received from their Japanese captors. As a tribute to the gallantry and bravery of the American and Philippine Forces, the Philippine government erected a huge towering 60-foot cross on Mount Samat.

Corregidor Island

"The Rock" as it was commonly called during World War II, is the location for the Pacific War Memorial. This was the island fortress where big guns defended the entrance to Manila Bay. A tour includes the Malinta Tunnel, which served as headquarters for General MacArthur and his staff. A light and sound display in the tunnel simulate conditions when the island was under siege by Japanese Forces. There are a number of memorials throughout the island. The most recent honors American Military Women who served under extreme hardship and earned the title "Angels Of Bataan and Corregidor." It was dedicated on May 6, 2000.

Subic Bay and Clark Field

Subic Bay was formerly the home for 50 years to the largest U.S. Navy Base outside the United States before it closed in 1992. It is now a bustling economic and commercial zone and resort. Clark Field was an American Air Base before and during World War II. After the Japanese occupation, it became Clark Field Concentration Camp and housed American prisoners of war who performed forced labor. After the devastating eruption of Mount Pinatubo in June 1991, most of the base was damaged. It is presently undergoing massive renovation and construction and will soon have a modern international airport. A first-class hotel and golf resort receives visitors to the former air base.

Manila American Cemetery and Memorial

This peaceful, well-manicured, final resting place of American veterans who fought in the Pacific is located near the center of Manila. It covers 152 acres of gently rising ground, which culminates at the Memorial. This is the biggest of cemeteries built and administered by the American Battle Monuments Commission. It contains the most graves of all national cemeteries along with actual listing of those Missing-In-Action. Their names are recorded on the walls of the Memorial.

Baguio City. Mountain Province

This city is the former location of the Camp John Hay Air Base. This American base was used for rest and recreation. The pristine area served as the summer capital of the Philippines. During World War 11, the 32nd Army Division gave hot pursuit and subsequently defeated the Japanese Forces headed by General Homma, the brutal commander of the Japanese Invasion Forces. Baguio City has the Philippine Military Academy, patterned after the U.S. Army Academy at West Point.

VFP Museum, Library, Archives, and Theatre

World War II history comes alive in this fantastic museum with state-of-the-art technology. Docu-dramas with stereo sounds highlight untold stories of heroism and daring acts of courage. Vividly recreated battle scenes are brought to life by dramatic lighting, narrations, and special effects. The excitement of battle is portrayed as American and Philippine soldiers take on the Japanese invaders. Audio-visual facilities show rare documentaries on World War II.

~ From the Philippine Department of Tourism

A Special Eulogy In Part for Major Richard Gordon, a Battling Bastard of Bataan who triggered the movement for a monument to the 1,600 Americans who perished on the Bataan Death March and died in July 2003, by Joseph R. Auriemma:

Somewhere in one of the great rooms of Heaven ...
there is a reunion today.

Hundreds, maybe thousands of American and Filipino soldiers who gave the ultimate sacrifice while fighting in the Philippines; those who died in battle; those who died while walking without food and water on the Bataan Death March; those who died of disease in the prison camps of O'Donnell and Cabanatuan, those who died aboard Hell Ships headed for camps outside the Philippines.

All have gathered to welcome another hero. In addition to saying "Welcome Richard. We suffered through Hell so we could see Heaven," I am sure they are saying . . . THANK YOU, RICHARD. Thank you for keeping the memory of our sacrifice alive.

I am sure that in most eulogies one would never hear what I am going to say about my friend, Richard.

Richard Gordon was a Bastard. He proudly told everyone that he was!

He was one of the Battling Bastards of Bataan. A title that soldiers themselves coined when they felt that their own government had forgotten them.

"We are the battling bastards of Bataan,
No mama, no papa, no Uncle Sam;
No aunts, no uncles, no cousins, no nieces;
No pills, no planes, no artillery pieces;
And nobody gives a damn.

Richard spent 3 ½ years as a Japanese prisoner of war. He saw atrocities that would make all of us ill.

With all this, it always amazed me that Richard held no animosity toward the people of Japan . . . just his captors.

ABOUT THE AUTHOR

DAN MURR

A colorful 42-year newspaper career ended in 1994. As a sport's writer, his journey carried him to many places, into many stadiums from the Big Ten to the Southeastern Conference, even to Notre Dame, to pro football and major league baseball. But he always had a deep burning desire to be a published author. It finally happened in 2000 when his first military adventure, A Need to Know, was published. In 2001, it won first place in published fiction from the Florida Writers Association.

He spent his best years as a sports editor/columnist at The Beacon-News in Aurora, Illinois (1979-1990), and at The Journal-Gazette in Fort Wayne Indiana (1976-78). Other stops included The Reflector, Norwalk, Ohio, The Lorain Journal, Florida Times-Union, Jacksonville, FL, St. Augustine Record, and Gainesville Sun.

His writing career continued after he retired with We Never Said Goodbye (and other stories); The Medjugorje Encounter, his second military adventure, The Milk Wagon, and The Sabbatine Privilege. Now comes his most prized work of . . . But Deliver Us from Evil, the true story of U.S. Army Chaplain John E. Duffy, who suvived the Bataan Death March and after World War II, became the pastor of Our Lady of Lourdes Catholic Church in Dan's hometown of New London, Ohio.

Dan now lives in Jacksonville Beach, Florida with his wife, Celeste, and two miniature Schnauzers, Maggie and Mitzie, and he continues on his writing road.

Books by Dan Murr

Fiction:

A Need to Know

The Milk Wagon

We Never Said Goodbye (and other stories)

The Sabbatine Privilege

Nonfiction:

The Medjugorje Encounter

...But Deliver Us from Evil:
Father Duffy and the Men of Bataan

CPSIA information can be obtained
at www.ICGtesting.com
Printed in the USA
LVOW12s1154091017

551748LV00001B/159/P